Spanish
Pathways

Marc Simmons

Spanish Pathways

READINGS IN THE HISTORY
OF HISPANIC NEW MEXICO

Marc Simmons

UNIVERSITY OF NEW MEXICO PRESS
ALBUQUERQUE

Library of Congress Cataloging-in-Publication Data:

Simmons, Marc.
Spanish pathways : readings in the history of Hispanic New Mexico /
Marc Simmons.— 1st ed.
p. cm.
Includes bibliographical references (p.) and index.
ISBN 0-8263-2373-1 (cloth : alk. paper) —
ISBN 0-8263-2374-X (paper : alk. paper)
1. Hispanic Americans—New Mexico—History.
2. Hispanic Americans—New Mexico—Social conditions.
3. Hispanic Americans—New Mexico—Social life and customs.
4. New Mexico—History.
5. New Mexico—Social life and customs.
6. New Mexico—Ethnic relations.
I. Title.
F805.S75 S56 2001
978.9'00468073—dc21   2001000947

All illustrations are from the author's collection unless otherwise noted.

CONTENTS

DEDICATED TO THE MEMORY OF
SAMUEL McC. GOODWIN
BRIG. GEN., U.S. ARMY, RET.

PREFACE

NOT SO LONG AGO, social history had less standing than political, diplomatic, or constitutional history—the departments of the past that deal with great events and profound movements that swept across decades, or even centuries. The commonplace things of everyday life furnishing the raw materials for a study of social history were looked down upon by many historians engaged in sophisticated and complex analysis of the weighty affairs of national politics and the rise and fall of entire civilizations.

More recently, a shift in attitude has led to the widespread belief that the way average citizens lived, worked, played, and worshipped has had a profound impact on the direction taken by history's currents. In fact, the pursuit of social history has now become not only respectable, but fashionable. Fortunately, that field is so wide and offers so many opportunities for scholarly exploration that research remains an adventure, like any journey of discovery.

Hispanic New Mexico, beginning with its founding in the sixteenth century, is an exceedingly rich field for social historians attracted by the activities and behavior of an exotic people, set against a dramatic landscape. In stark contrast to the glittering opulence of the viceregal capital of Mexico City, the poor and bedraggled New Mexican capital at the very end of the Camino Real appeared for much of its early existence to be a place forsaken by man and God.

Tiny Santa Fe, nestled at the foot of the majestic Sangre de Cristo Mountains, lacked most of the amenities available in provincial cities elsewhere in Spanish America. Its plaza and streets were dusty in summer and ankle-deep in mud during the snowy season. Residences and churches, built for utility of unfired adobe bricks, lacked any hint of elegance. Even the flat-roofed Governor's Palace facing the plaza had no trace of grandeur about it. Almost everything in Santa Fe, and other New Mexican towns and villages, was rustic in the extreme.

Supporting this frontier society was an economy based mainly on subsistence farming and ranching, but including exports of livestock on the hoof; wool and rough textiles; leather goods; buffalo jerky, hides, and tallow; piñon nuts; and salt. Economic development, beyond this simple structure, proved difficult, owing to the isolation of the province, environmental impediments, and chronic problems with hostile Indians.

In my earlier book, *Coronado's Land, Daily Life in Colonial New Mexico* (University of New Mexico Press, 1991), I presented a series of sketches for the general reader that treated some of the picturesque, but quite fundamental, aspects of domestic living among the Hispanic New Mexicans. The chapters in the present work are longer, run deeper in detail, and include scholarly citations. All but two ("Colonial Physicians" and "St. John's Day") have been published before in professional journals.

As in the previous book, these assembled articles bear upon New Mexico's social and economic history. They should prove of interest to a more specialized readership—students, researchers, and lay persons who are perhaps as fascinated with the long march of Southwestern history as I have always been.

Although some of these pieces were published early in my career, I believe that all of them have held up well over the years and that as a collection they continue to help our understanding of the mercurial New Mexican past. They support two conclusions confirmed by the most recent research of other scholars.

First is the recognition that the society and the economy on the upper Rio Grande were far more complex and deeply textured than was formerly believed. And second, traditional Hispanic life on this frontier was shaped by pervasive poverty and abiding misfortune, which are often found in an economic backwater where under-development is endemic. Out of those unenviable conditions, the New Mexicans fashioned their own formulas for survival, becoming in the process resilient and stoic. Their achievement, in the face of harsh realities, is worthy of our admiration.

Readers will observe some small variation in the citation form within my endnotes, reflecting the differences in style-requirements of the publications in which these chapters originally appeared. For them in most cases, new or shortened titles have been created for this book. The journals in which the articles first appeared are identified in the Acknowledgments at the back of the volume. A brief explanatory text in italics precedes each chapter.

I am pleased to have this opportunity, provided by the University of New Mexico Press, to pull together this material under a single cover, thereby making it more accessible. I hope it aids a writer someday in the production of a comprehensive survey of the social and economic side of New Mexico's engaging history.

Marc Simmons
Cerrillos, New Mexico

INTRODUCTION

F ROM its initial settlement in 1598 until Mexican independence from Spain in 1821, New Mexico played a pivotal role in the support and defense of the vast northern rim of the Viceroyalty of New Spain. Although isolated on the far frontier, colonial settlers of the province maintained a strong sense of Hispanidad and a deep attachment to political, social, and religious institutions that had originated in the mother country. At public ceremonies New Mexicans shouted *huzzas* for their king, a remote and shadowy figure who symbolized the paternalism of the Spanish Empire. But it was the viceroy, the Crown's chief administrative officer in Mexico City, who bore direct responsibility for management of the province. To him the governor and people of New Mexico looked for solutions to the many problems that plagued day-to-day existence on the upper Rio Grande, so that in time they developed a feeling of identity that partook as much of the New World as it did of the Old.

Spain transferred not only her chief governmental and social institutions to the colonies but also a selective assortment of agricultural products and techniques, art and craft traditions, and other skills and customs. Iberian culture underwent significant modification in central Mexico as it came under influences from a distinctive environment and the lifeways of a large Native American population. By the time cultural baggage from Spain was repackaged and shipped northward hundreds of miles to New Mexico, part of the original consignment had been filtered out and much of the remainder had taken on a uniquely Mexican flavor. Notwithstanding, the underlying character and tone of life on the Rio Grande frontier remained unquestionably Hispanic.

Don Juan de Oñate, a creole (Spaniard born in America), founded New Mexico's first community and the provincial capital at San Gabriel, on the Rio Grande adjacent to San Juan Pueblo, in 1598. Before coming to the new province, Oñate's colonizing expedition was subjected to a meticulous review by the royal inspector, Juan de Frías Salazar, to determine whether the supplies were sufficient and in proper order. The inventories compiled by Salazar indicate that in addition to livestock and agricultural seed the expedition carried manufactured articles of considerable variety and quantity. Such goods included finished hardware, clothing, weapons, medicine, religious items, glass beads, books and paper, mining equipment, and tools for craftsmen. With these material belongings the Spaniards expected to build and furnish homes, workshops, and missions and to supply their daily needs until the colony became well established.[1]

The men and women with Oñate were a proud and aristocratic lot. A few, the record shows, possessed special skills like those of carpenter and gunsmith. One individual even seems to have been versed in the practice of medicine. On the whole, however, most appear to have been recruited from among the mining gentry of New Spain, a class with little talent and less inclination for manual labor. Their great desire in coming north was to discover a silver mine and make a quick personal fortune.

The colonists arrived in New Mexico intending to recreate some semblance of the elegant society to which they had grown accustomed earlier in central Mexico or Spain. Salazar's documents show that many of them brought articles of fine apparel, tailored of silk and velvet, and richly ornamented horse trappings suitable for ceremonial processions and parades. These Spaniards, so fond of public display and marks of status, persisted for a time in their noble pretensions, but finally the difficult and abiding realities of the New Mexico frontier obliged them to make practical adaptations in daily life. Suits and dresses of imported fabric largely gave way to ones made of coarse homespun cloth and leather. Homemade saddles and bridles replaced the resplendent horse equipage which had little functional use in the absence of showy parades. The luxury items represented a way of life left behind, and their eventual casting off suggested a new willingness on the part of the New Mexicans to meet the pioneering experience on its own terms.

Soon after his arrival Oñate discovered that the wagonloads of supplies, paid for at his own expense, were not going to be enough to see the colonists through their first lean years on the Rio Grande. Therefore he addressed a letter to the crown asking that additional provisions be issued to him. In response, a caravan set out for New Mexico in 1600 bearing all manner of staples, but including also cast iron bedsteads and Spanish cordovan shoes.[2] That wagon train, financed by the royal treasury, was but the first of many in the seventeenth century that took the dust-laden Camino Real north-ward to the struggling, supply-starved colony of New Mexico.

In 1609, the same year that plans were formulated for the found-ing of Santa Fe, the Spanish government assumed full responsibility for the support and maintenance of the Franciscan missions scattered among the Indian pueblos. As a result, it decided to send a train of supplies from Mexico City once every three years to stock the storerooms of the New Mexico missions. For the first twenty years or so, however, the supply caravan did not keep its schedule, mainly due to bureaucratic red tape and indifference; consequently, arrivals were often five and six years apart. The delays worked a severe hardship on the missionary program and prompted strong protests from the friars.

With continued expansion of the church's work, supply service expenses mounted steadily. The 1629 caravan, for example, cost the treasury 81,000 pesos. In an effort to hold down expenditures and improve delivery, royal authorities and officials of the Franciscan Order agreed to reorganize the caravan system on a more formal and

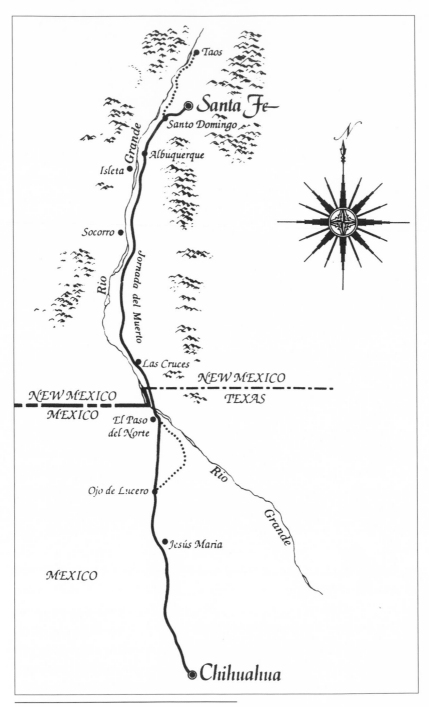

Map of Camino Real.
Used by permission of the Camino Real Project

efficient basis. The plan called for designating an experienced friar as "Procurator-General" who would serve as supply agent and wagon-master with complete authority to provision the Rio Grande missions. The formal contract under which this agent operated specified that he receive sixty thousand pesos for the purchase and shipment of goods, that he have thirty-two wagons and five hundred mules at his disposal, and that his caravan be furnished with a military escort. After inauguration of these procedures in 1631, the freighting service demonstrated conspicuous improvement, most noticeably in the prompt arrival of the supply caravan every three years.

The standard list of supplies, the Procurator-General's buying guide, contained almost two hundred separate classes of items to be purchased for New Mexico. Among the articles were Rouen cloth from France, Spanish almonds and olive oil, Chinese damask, and axes made on the street of the ironworkers in Mexico City.[3] The large imports of foodstuffs and manufactured goods introduced in the decades before 1680 allowed the missions to flourish and exude an air of prosperity. But the relative plenty enjoyed by the friars was not shared in by the majority of colonists.

The government, weighed down with the financial burden of the church, could offer little in the way of material support for the settlers. That elicited complaints, notably from the *cabildo*, or municipal council, of Santa Fe, that Spaniards suffered in poverty while newly Christianized Indians received abundant aid through the missions. Although such charges were often exaggerated, they also bore a grain of truth.

New Mexico's feeble economy in the period 1600 to 1680 was subsidized not only by the treasury's assistance to the missionary program but also by tribute payments which the Pueblo Indians were forced to make under the *encomienda* system. Annually each native household paid tribute in corn and cotton blankets, amounting in effect to a tax diverted to the use of the Hispanic community. These enforced collections offset to some extent the material benefits which the Indians received from the missions.

With a Spanish population of perhaps 2,500 by the 1670s, the province was essentially rural in character, with Santa Fe, its capital, being the only formally organized municipality. *Estancias*—large landed estates composed of irrigated farmland along the Rio Grande or its tributaries and pasture on adjacent tablelands—constituted the principal units of economic enterprise. Cottage industry was only weakly developed, although several corrupt governors at Santa Fe operated illegal sweatshops, called *obrajes*. There they used impressed Indian labor to produce blankets and stockings which the governors exported to the mining communities of northern New Spain and sold for personal profit.[4]

In the aftermath of the Pueblo revolt and reconquest, 1680 to 1696, new economic patterns and institutions emerged. Besides destroying the great estates and forcing discontinuance of the encomienda or tribute system, the tumult had dealt a severe blow to Spanish pride. New settlers recruited from Zacatecas and other points in central Mexico by Governor Diego de Vargas were primarily small farmers and artisans who, unlike the earlier Oñate colonists, harbored no illusions about the kind of life they would find on the New Mexico frontier. Even so, difficulties proved formidable, at least in the beginning. Vargas's successor, Francisco Cuerbo y Valdés, writing to the king of Spain early in 1706, declared dejectedly: "I have never seen so much want, misery, and backwardness in my life. I suspect this land was better off before the Spaniards came."[5] Such a candid admission from a political officer was rare.

One conspicuous change was evident in the transportation system. The mission supply service operated by the Franciscans was abandoned sometime before the middle of the eighteenth century. It was replaced by government caravans managed by private contractors who conveyed consignments of goods destined for the friars, soldiers in the newly established Santa Fe presidio, and citizens at large.

Another new development was apparent in eighteenth-century land use patterns. The large estates which had once dominated the rural landscape declined in importance. Perhaps reflecting that fact, the old term "estancia" was discarded (or at least it was no longer used in contemporary documents) and seems to have been replaced by the word "hacienda." While there was some clustering of sizable estates in the Río Abajo (that is, in the middle Rio Grande Valley south of Santa Fe), throughout most of the province the *rancho*, or small privately owned farm, came to predominate.

Still another significant feature during the post-revolt era was the rise of new urban centers at Santa Cruz de la Cañada north of Santa Fe, at Albuquerque, and at El Paso del Norte, which was then within the jurisdiction of New Mexico. All three, together with the capital, were ranked as *villas*, a prestigious title accorded important Spanish towns. Taos also aspired to villa status but failed to achieve it under the colonial regime.

During the eighteenth century New Mexico's Spanish population showed a steady if unspectacular growth, surpassing 11,000 in 1760 and reaching nearly 24,000 by the year 1800.[6] Although the mainstays of the provincial economy remained subsistence farming and stock raising, the expanding Hispanic community increasingly offered new avenues for making a livelihood. Indian trading and buffalo hunting engaged scores of men at certain seasons of the year. Trade with the Chihuahua markets attracted others. Most communities, large and small, boasted a fair number of millers who operated primitive gristmills on streams or irrigation ditches. A few New Mexicans engaged in copper mining and even smelted the ore and produced "wrought copper vessels of superior quality" for export, or so Lieutenant Zebulon Pike claimed on his trip down the Rio Grande in 1806.[7]

Wool growing in the Río Abajo led to the rise of a small weaving industry at Albuquerque, where independent weavers produced blankets, *jerga* (rough floor covering), and *sabanilla* (wool sheeting) for both local consumption and the Chihuahua trade. As early as 1744, Francisco de Vargas, the *mayordomo* of a large mule train from Mexico City, journeyed to Albuquerque for the express purpose of purchasing surplus wool. He was acting as agent for a wealthy merchant of the viceregal capital, but what is significant was that he traveled all the way to New Mexico to make his purchases.[8] A round trip from Mexico City to Albuquerque could be made much faster

*Weaving of rough textiles on heavy looms such
as this one was an important cottage industry
in colonial New Mexico.*
Museum of New Mexico photograph neg. no. 22681

with a pack train than with ox carts, but even so such a journey required five to six months.

The extensive 1790 census of New Mexico lists Albuquerque citizens employed in more than thirty different occupations. Besides weavers and carders, they were blacksmiths, silversmiths, carpenters, masons, tailors, tanners, cobblers, hatters, teachers, musicians, muleteers, and merchants. Unfortunately, in most cases little is known about the methods of work and products of those who were craftsmen and artisans.[9]

Extant documentary evidence shows that occasionally workmen who emigrated to New Mexico were master smiths, tailors, and carpenters, having attained that rank after undergoing rigorous examination by the craft guilds (*gremios*) of Mexico City, Puebla, and other central Mexican cities. The guild system itself, which had originated in Spain, was not transferred to New Mexico. According to Governor Fernando de Chacón's economic report of 1803: "With regard to craft organizations, it can properly be said that none exist in this province since there is no instruction nor examination for the office of master, or formal guilds, nor all the rest which is customary elsewhere."[10]

The governor's denial of any craft instruction is too sweeping, for it is known that accomplished artisans occasionally accepted apprentices for a term specified by formal contract.[11] Apparently too, fathers regularly instructed their sons in the ways of the family shop, as was the case, for example, with the Senas of Santa Fe who for more than two centuries passed the craft of blacksmithing from generation to generation.

New Mexican artisans and craftsmen drew on a rich heritage of Hispanic material culture in designing the utilitarian and decorative products needed in the province. The overriding influence, of course, derived from the mother country's Spanish-Moorish tradition. It provided the framework within which the distinctive matrix of New Mexican culture evolved and to which in time were added elements from the Indians of central Mexico, the Indians of the Southwest, and even influences from the Andes and the Far East.

Nevertheless, whatever his occupation, the colonial New Mexican found his sense of identity and defined the parameters of daily life through a firm allegiance to the Spanish state and the Spanish church—the "Two Majesties," as they were popularly called. Reverence for the empire and the sovereign and faith in the Catholic Church were sentiments the people of New Mexico shared in full measure with other inhabitants of the viceroyalty. As late as the first quarter of the nineteenth century, New Mexicans repeatedly responded with donations whenever the king indicated he was in financial need or the Spanish church asked for special contributions to support nunneries and similar pious institutions in the Iberian Peninsula.

One trait possessed by New Mexico's citizens and often commented upon by visitors from Mexico City was their strong sense of individualism which made them restive under the stiff controls imposed by the very state and church that commanded their devoted loyalty. When Santa Fe citizens resisted an order issued by Governor Fernando de la Concha in 1788, he complained to his superiors in Mexico about the Santa Feans' "churlish nature" and condemned "the perfect freedom in which they have always lived."[12] A decade before, Father Morfi had likewise indicted New Mexicans for being undisciplined and for preferring to live on their own, in remote areas, rather than congregating in towns.[13]

Another characteristic of New Mexicans that attracted notice was their bravery, particularly while conducting campaigns against hostile Indians. Settlers all along the northern rim of New Spain seem to have exhibited an individualistic temperament and abundant courage. By contrast, the masses of peasants in central Mexico, much given to communal enterprise, appeared docile and passive. To a large degree, the difference may well be attributed to the dangers and hardships on a frontier where the rigorous struggle for survival promoted the qualities of personal initiative, endurance, and independence.

The flow of material goods and ideas northward to the upper Rio Grande from the Viceroyalty of New Spain accelerated in the second half of the eighteenth century. While the society that had evolved on the Rio Grande has frequently been described as self-sufficient and provincial, it was not entirely so. New Mexico's isolation was more apparent than actual, since a continuing stream of new settlers, government officials, missionaries, merchants, and soldiers provided contact, however tenuous, with the mainstream of Hispanic culture. The Camino Real linked New Mexico to the seat of viceregal authority in Mexico City, to the high court, or *audiencia*, of Guadalajara, and to Durango, residence of the bishop who exercised episcopal jurisdiction over the north central provinces. In addition, especially during the later colonial years, New Mexicans increasingly took the road south to trade at some of the booming regional fairs at a number of frontier cities and towns.

The prime focus of economic activity in New Mexico during later colonial times was the annual trade fairs, which brought together Spaniards, Pueblos, and assorted nomadic tribesmen. By the 1790s major fairs were designed to cater to a single tribe, since government officials had concluded that keeping the groups apart reduced the chance of hostilities while the trading was in progress. Thus, the Taos fair drew the Comanche; those at Santa Clara and Santa Fe, the Ute; while the Pecos fairs served the Jicarilla Apache (and on some alternate occasions, the Comanche). The Navajo attended fairs at Jemez and Acoma, the Mescalero Apache those at El Paso del Norte. Of all these the Taos fair was the grandest, most popular and largest in volume of business.

The fairs of Taos, although frequently mentioned by scholars in general terms, have never been studied in the detail that they deserve. As social and economic institutions, fairs had far-reaching consequences for the history of colonial New Mexico; they also constitute one of the more romantic chapters of that story.

According to the first Spaniards, the Pueblo people had no true fairs or markets, which meant that they lacked public places where barter was carried on at a prearranged time. Nevertheless, the inhabitants of Taos, Picuris, Pecos and other pueblos did conduct an informal trade with the Plains Apaches whenever bands bearing merchandise put in an appearance. The variety of commodities was quite limited; farming Indians exchanged maize and cotton blankets for dried meat and hides brought by the Plains people.

During the seventeenth century both Taos and Pecos began to emerge as primary trade centers, in large part due to their location on the frontier and accessibility to the nomads. But it was not until 1723 that a Spanish royal decree officially established annual fairs at both places. The decree was issued in response to reports that French traders from Louisiana were wandering among the tribes of the southern plains. The Crown hoped that the appeal of annual fairs in New Mexico would lure the nomad Indians into Spain's commercial orbit and cement their loyalty and friendship.

From the beginning Taos was the fair that attracted the most attention, undoubtedly because it was the one attended by the Comanches, whose wealth and power were unrivaled. Initially the event was scheduled in July or August, the exact date, according to Fray Manuel Trigo, being set by the changes of the moon.[14] The governor, or in his place the lieutenant governor, often participated, as did many New Mexican colonists and soldiers. The governor's presence was most useful since he helped to preserve order and to curb the tendency of his subjects to engage in cheating when transacting business with the Indians.

Matters pertaining to the fair were strictly regulated. Spanish citizens, for instance, were forbidden to trade with the Comanches outside the period specified for the fair. One citizen, Diego de Torres, who tried to get a jump on his competitors in 1735 by trading some buffalo robes from the Comanche prior to the official date, was taken to court where everything he had obtained from the Indians was ordered confiscated.[15]

By all accounts the Comanches who ventured to Taos were a wild and unruly lot, much given to revelry and uninhibited displays of passion. Friars who witnessed the noisy pageantry of the fair described it as a drunken debauchery that aided the cause of Satan. Of greater concern was the fact that while some Comanches were conducting peaceful barter at Taos, other members of the tribe were carrying out devastating raids elsewhere in the province. Since the Middle Ages Spaniards had been accustomed to observe a "Truce of

*Modern re-enactors, with dress
and arms typical of Spaniards in
sixteenth-century New Mexico.*

God" guaranteeing the safety of everyone going to and from a fair. The Plains Indians had a similar custom, and so the Comanches were able to do business at Taos even in those years when their war with the colonists was at its peak.

Spanish efforts to defend New Mexico from Comanche incursions were many and costly. In 1747 Governor Joaquín Codallos y Rabal set out with a campaign force of five hundred men and fought the Comanche and their Ute allies in a battle near Abiquiu. A few months later he had another encounter with the Comanches at Pecos Pueblo. Notwithstanding, when the Taos fair opened in mid 1748, the governor gave a friendly reception to six hundred members of the tribe when they assured him that they had played no part in the recent hostilities.

The viceroy thought that was going a little too far and ordered a junta to convene in Santa Fe to decide whether the Comanches should, henceforward, be allowed to participate in the Taos fair. As far as the New Mexicans were concerned the issue was never in doubt. At the junta they concluded that the Comanche trade was vital to the economy of the province and that it should be continued despite the tribe's unreliable and treacherous character.[16]

The incongruous situation—Spaniards blandly doing business with enemy Comanches for the duration of the Taos fair—dragged on until 1786 when Governor Juan Bautista de Anza negotiated a permanent peace with the Indians. In the same year Viceroy Bernardo de Gálvez issued a set of instructions to frontier governors urging them to encourage and develop trade with all tribes since, as he put it: "The interest in commerce binds and narrows the desires of man."[17] By that he meant that once the Indians had become economically dependent upon the Spaniards they would be more apt to keep peace treaties so as not to disrupt their source of goods.

How to control the Indians and how to promote the provincial economy were two of the main questions concerning New Mexico that engaged the attention of the royal government. It also had to face the threat posed by foreigners from the East—first the French and then Anglo-Americans late in the eighteenth century—all anxious to open trade with the New Mexican settlements. Spain was rigidly opposed to this, both because she feared foreigners might subvert the loyalty of her colonial subjects and because she wished to keep a tight monopoly over all commerce within the borders of the empire. As a result, the Crown issued a series of laws effectively closing the northern frontier of New Spain to any form of intercolonial trade.

The tight monopolistic policy forced New Mexicans to purchase all their manufactured goods in Chihuahua and its neighboring provinces where prices were high owing to transportation costs from the principal seaports. Buyers from the Rio Grande also found to their dismay that southern merchants routinely inflated prices and resorted to other sharp practices whenever a wagon train from New Mexico arrived. The result, according to Father Juan Agustín de Morfí in 1778, was that "there is scarcely any margin with which the New Mexicans can pay freight and still support themselves even at a poverty level. Since they have no alternative, they are forced to accept the rules laid down in Chihuahua."[18]

Some relief came later in the same century and in the early years of the following century with establishment of new fairs in northern Mexico. These gave the Rio Grande merchants added chances to seek competitive prices. The most prominent of such fairs were the ones at San Juan de los Lagos in Nueva Galicia, San Juan del Río in Durango, Saltillo in Coahuila, and the Valle de San Bartolomé south of Chihuahua City, which was not begun until 1806.[19]

All the fairs enjoyed the *libertad de derechos*, that is, exemption from burdensome duties such as the *derecho de consumo* (consumption tax) and the *alcabala* (sales tax) which were ordinarily levied on goods each time they changed hands. The tax-free period during the official days of the fair served to attract participants from afar, and stimulated business.

The Taos fair has often been described in terms of the wide Plains Indian trade, but little note has been taken of the numerous Spanish merchants who traveled long distances from the south to take part. Taos, the oldest and among the most prestigious of frontier fairs, formed part of a network of fairs operating on a seasonal cycle. By a strict scheduling that allowed an appropriate interval between fairs participants were able to move expeditiously from one to the other, transporting newly acquired merchandise by mule train or ox cart.[20] This system was also fed by European goods funneled through the annual Jalapa fair (which dispersed shipments introduced into the nearby Gulf port of Veracruz) and Asiatic and South American wares, particularly textiles and ceramics, brought to the Acapulco fair by Pacific galleons.[21]

Unfortunately, the paucity of records makes it impossible either to calculate the volume of trade carried on at the Taos fair or to gauge the impact on provincial society and culture which the annual influx of outside merchants must have had. At the very least, it can be said that the fair exerted considerable influence on New Mexico's economic and cultural configuration. At the same time it served as an important bond tying the remote upper Rio Grande Valley to the Viceroyalty of New Spain.

New Mexico's lifeline to the south was the Camino Real, a road which originated at Taos, extended through Santa Fe, Albuquerque, and El Paso to the main commercial centers of New Spain, and ended in Mexico City. Annual convoys of merchant wagons, replacing the earlier mission supply service, traveled this route and provided the means for an interchange of goods and ideas. The organization and management of these convoys, called *conductas*, form an intriguing chapter in the early economic history of the Southwest.

The New Mexicans usually went south once a year in a single large convoy protected by an escort of regular soldiers and militiamen. Besides wagon and pack animals in the caravan, thousands of head of sheep were taken to be sold in the mining communities of northern New Spain. Five hundred persons was considered the minimum number needed to insure safe passage through the country of hostile Apaches.[22]

At first the convoys operated on no fixed schedule, although once a date for departure was decided upon it was announced well in advance. On October 12, 1732, for example, the New Mexican governor directed *alcaldes* (district magistrates) to inform their citizens that the annual conducta would leave for Mexico the following November 1. Those with goods or livestock to sell were instructed to rendezvous at Albuquerque. The governor also reminded the alcaldes that everyone who planned to go was obliged to obtain a travel permit, one of the many petty restrictions imposed upon Spanish subjects.[23]

Later in the 1700s the rendezvous point was shifted downriver to the village of La Joya, and the time for the caravan departure was set soon after the close of the Taos fair in midsummer. After the fair date was moved to the fall the convoy left at its conclusion, usually in late October or early November. That enabled the New Mexican merchants to make the fifty-day journey to the fair of San Bartolomé in time for its opening on December 18. The fair, established by a viceregal decree of February 24, 1806, was aimed primarily at promoting and encouraging commerce from the province of New Mexico.[24]

Besides their important economic function, the trade convoys also had significant social ramifications. The merchants often took their entire families on the trail, since that was far safer than leaving them at home, unprotected and at the mercy of the Indians. The caravans thus became traveling societies in miniature and were witness to births, marriages, and deaths.

Convoys returning from Chihuahua provided the principal means by which new settlers reached the upper Rio Grande. They included such persons as peasant farmers, artisans, and retired soldiers who for a variety of reasons had decided to immigrate to New Mexico. Moreover, government officials, military officers, and friars newly assigned to the province customarily joined the northbound convoy, enjoying the safety if afforded travelers.

In 1812 Pedro Bautista Pino recounted the mode of operation for the Spanish caravans, which had evolved over the previous century. At the rendezvous point food and water barrels were assembled, inspections conducted, and assignments made for the horseguard and the sentries who, in Pino's words, "on dark nights are to listen for footsteps by putting their ear to the ground and thus to prevent the surprise attacks which have often occurred."[25]

Although merchants came from all parts of New Mexico, the largest number seems to have been concentrated in the Río Abajo, especially in the Albuquerque-Bernalillo district. They probably cannot be referred to as a distinct occupational class since the overland trade was a seasonal pursuit. Most, if not all, New Mexicans involved in commerce also carried on their own farming and ranching enterprises.

When barriers to foreign trade were dismantled following Mexican independence in 1821, and the first American merchants entered the region, they no doubt took note of the tightly structured convoy system governing traffic on the Camino Real. It seems likely that the Spanish model furnished at least some inspiration for the regimen of caravans subsequently developed on the Santa Fe Trail and described in the classic accounts by Josiah Gregg, Matthew Field, and others.

Throughout the 225 years of the colonial period, and indeed through the quarter-century of Mexican rule (1821–1846), New Mexico remained essentially a frontier zone. That meant that Indian raids and desperate struggles to make a living became a way of life; the security and prosperity won by Anglo-American pioneers on the eastern frontier after a generation or two continually eluded Hispanic folk on the Rio Grande. Out of the crucible of their frontier experience, the New Mexicans developed a regional culture admirably fitted to the time and place, and in so doing demonstrated an equanimity of spirit and a remarkable physical resiliency. ∞

CHAPTER ONE

THE PUEBLO REVOLT: WHY DID IT HAPPEN?

The Pueblo Indians' expulsion of the Spaniards from New Mexico in 1680 stands as a major landmark in the history of the Borderlands frontier. Owing to the heavy casualties on both sides and to the more than two decades of bloody turmoil that followed, the event can be viewed as a calamity for each side alike.

The Pueblo success marked a humiliating defeat for the Spanish Empire, one of the worst ever experienced in its New World colonies. The long-range consequences of the revolt would be studied by historians one day, but the immediate causes the Spaniards themselves began to examine even before the smoke of battle had cleared. What they found and whom they blamed for their loss forms an interesting commentary on Spanish thinking in the late seventeenth century.

N EW MEXICO'S great Indian revolt of 1680 was the product of multiple influences that had their roots in the eight decades prior to that year. On August 10, a vast web of interlocking forces converged and touched off a spectacularly successful rebellion by the Pueblo people of the upper Rio Grande Valley who had been smarting under Spanish rule since the close of the sixteenth century.

It was, as many writers have pointed out, the first successful battle for independence fought against a European colonial power in what was to become the United States.

As early as 1650, during the administration of Governor Hernando de Ugarte y la Concha, several of the southern Pueblo towns, between Isleta and Cochiti, conspired with friendly Apaches to launch a war against the Spaniards and drive them from the land. The plot, however, was discovered, nine native leaders were hanged, and many other persons were sold into slavery. But from that time forward, the royal authorities were constantly beset with rumors of new conspiracies and threats of a general uprising.

The underlying cause of tension between Spaniard and Pueblo in this period can be found in the religious attitudes brought to New Mexico by the Franciscan friars and colonists. They came not only with the ingrained belief in the superiority of Hispanic Catholicism but also with the firm conviction that other faiths should be banished, by force if necessary. There was no way the Spanish mind of the seventeenth century could accept the coexistence of Christianity and the "pagan practices" of the Pueblos. The friars' single-minded dedication to the eradication of all aspects of Pueblo ceremonialism is underscored by the ferocity they showed in destroying, with the aid of soldiers, the sacred kivas and ritual objects, such as fetishes and kachina masks.

Religious persecution was something wholly new to the Pueblos and it left them utterly bewildered. Unlike the Europeans who felt

A Pueblo Indian leader with his bow and arrows.
Bureau of American Ethnology photograph

compelled to defend the exclusiveness of Christianity and proclaim it the sole path to spiritual truth, the Pueblo Indians have looked upon all religions as contributing to harmony in the cosmos. Initially, they were quite willing to accept the White Man's religion and integrate it into their own ceremonial structure. But the earliest Spanish padres would have none of that.

In the disruption of their dances and rituals by overzealous Spaniards, the Pueblos perceived the cause of several natural disasters that befell them in the decades prior to 1680. A devastating drought beginning in 1666 lasted five years. It produced widespread famine and led to the deaths of hundreds of Pueblos from starvation. Many survivors, weakened by the ordeal, succumbed to epidemic disease. The nomadic Apache, finding the wild game growing scarce during the era of drought, increasingly took to raiding Pueblo as well as Spanish communities in quests for food. Their growing hostility aggravated New Mexico's already desperate economic plight.

Assailed by such baleful woes, the Pueblo people concluded that Christianity was ineffectual in providing relief. The drought they blamed directly on the friars who had put a halt to the ancient rain-making ceremonies and thereby disrupted the delicate relationship between man and the native deities who governed the universe. Indeed, it is said that the Hopi stole away to some cliffs and secretly held the midsummer Niman Kachina rite, thereby producing rain. Christian prayer and services had failed to achieve a similar result, which was interpreted to mean that the religion of the Spaniards was of no use to the Indians.

In reflecting upon the Revolt, after the fact, both civil officials and missionaries were quick to assign a supernatural cause to the catastrophe. Initially, Antonio de Otermín, the governor in 1680, and Father Francisco de Ayeta, *visitador-general* of the Franciscan Order in New Mexico, both attributed the Revolt to their own "grievous sins." But upon calmer reflection, each man decided that the Devil, in truth, was to blame.

Because of what they termed the "stupid ignorance" and "stupid vices" of the Pueblos, Satan had been presented a sterling opportunity to bring down the Christian province of New Mexico. Curiously, the surviving friars mourned not their fellow missionaries who had been slain, but rather they lamented the loss of the many Pueblo souls that, because of the rebellion, were destined for Hell!

Plainly, the Spaniards were looking for a scapegoat to ease their own consciences and they found a handy and, to their minds, plausible one in the person of the Devil. The cabildo (the municipal council) of Santa Fe, while in flight southward to El Paso with the governor and other refugees, paused at the foot of the Fray Cristóbal Mountain below Socorro long enough to issue an *auto*, or formal statement on the Revolt. Therein, the officers declared with conviction that discord that the Devil had sown among the natives was the spark that set off the general rebellion.

It is interesting to note that Governor Otermín, during an unsuccessful attempt to reconquer New Mexico late in 1681, interviewed one of the original leaders of the uprising, Alonso Catití. According to his statement, Catití wept openly, kissed the feet of a priest, and repented, saying that the Devil had deceived them. Since that was exactly what the Governor wanted to hear, we have reason to hold suspect the accuracy of his reporting. (But it is, of course, possible that some of the Indian leadership had indeed invoked the aid of the Spaniards' Devil in formulating a plan for revolution.)

The native Pueblo religion, with its emphasis on public dancing, handling of venomous snakes, wearing of masks, and the sprinkling of sacred cornmeal, appeared so offensive to the mind of the seventeenth-century Spaniard that he could explain it only as a creation of Satan. Juan Domínguez de Mendoza, an officer with Otermín during the abortive reconquest of 1681, found a room filled with painted kachina masks in the abandoned pueblo of Sandia. Declared he, "Only with the aid of the Devil could they make such abominable figures." Wholly insensitive to the sacred nature of these objects, Domínguez promptly burned them.

Precisely it was the firing of kivas and the burning of ritual paraphernalia which had fueled the anger of the Pueblos before 1680. According to the later testimony of Revolt participants, they had

*Spanish violation of ceremonial
kivas such as this one led to the
Pueblo Revolt.*
Museum of New Mexico
photograph neg. no. 3693

spent their chief fury upon the churches, destroying them in retaliation for the burning of their own kivas. Similarly, they sought out and killed twenty-one Franciscan missionaries (about two-thirds of the total number of friars then stationed in New Mexico) to avenge the mistreatment accorded the *caciques*, the members of the Pueblo priesthood.

From the days of the earliest settlement in New Mexico, the Spanish clergy had condemned the caciques as sorcerers and servants of the Devil. Not surprisingly, these native priests became special objects of persecution. In 1675, four of them were hanged and forty-three others flogged after conviction on charges of practicing sorcery, communing with the Devil, and plotting with neighboring Apaches to rebel against the government.

As might be expected, the caciques took the lead in weaving the net of conspiracy which ultimately brought down the Spanish regime in New Mexico. Their motives were simple vengeance and a desire to see the restoration of pre-conquest religion and culture, which meant a return to their own unlimited authority in each village.

Among the common people, however, the sentiment for revolt seems to have been something less than universal. For that reason, the caciques evidently found it necessary to issue threats against persons showing timidity in joining. According to hearsay stories collected by the Spaniards, Indians known to be sympathetic to the Christian religion were assassinated on orders of the native priesthood. If that was true, then certainly the number of victims must have been comparatively small. What is clear, nevertheless, is that the Revolt started not among the masses, but at the top, among the priestly elite.

By all accounts, the religious leader Popé, a native of San Juan Pueblo, was the key figure in pulling together diverse factions among the Indians and forging a loose coalition capable of opposing the Spaniards.[1] He had been one of those condemned to the whipping post back in 1675. One widely believed story held that, in order to cement the unity necessary for victory, Popé traveled from one village to another on a whirlwind, a mode of transportation favored by sorcerers and witches. Royal officials also collected testimony to the effect that he claimed to be the personal spokesman and representative of *El Demonio*, the Devil.

In all of this can be seen the Spaniards' preoccupation with the supernatural as a primary cause of the calamitous Revolt. Less apparent to them at the time was the degree to which their physical abuse and general mistreatment of the Pueblos had aroused resentment and stirred up a spirit of resistance.

The friars had imposed swift and severe punishment for the slightest violation of religious duties. A whipping or a term in the stocks was the customary sentence. For a while at the beginning of the century, disobedient Indians had been subjected to a head-shaving. Loss of one's hair was regarded as a colossal indignity by the Pueblos, and some of them became so distraught, after the removal of their locks, that in humiliation they fled to the mountains. As a consequence, the royal government ordered that harsh bit of discipline stopped in 1620.

The colonists and civil officials, including the provincial governors, were also notorious abusers of the native people. When giving testimony in 1681 as to why the Revolt had occurred, one Pueblo witness asserted that it was because certain Spanish officials had beaten them, stolen from them, and made them work without pay. The two chief offenders were Francisco Xavier, New Mexico's royal secretary, and Alonso García, a high ranking military officer.

Under Spain's laws of the Indies, it was permissible to force Indians to work, both on public projects and on private farms and ranches. In all cases, however, they were to be paid at a fixed rate established by the government. But in New Mexico, that stipulation was violated with impunity, the colonists often imposing stiff labor demands on their Pueblo neighbors while neglecting to provide them any compensation.

One of the most frequent complaints of the Indians before the Revolt was that during those seasons of the year when they were most needed in their own fields, they were compelled to leave home and work the lands of the Spaniards. That hardship produced a decline in the size of the annual Pueblo harvest and reduced their reserves of foodstuffs to dangerously low levels. That became tragically apparent during the prolonged drought of the 1660s, when famine resulted in an unprecedented number of deaths.

A minority of Spaniards, mostly men of rank and influence, were in the habit of violating native women, a practice which fanned the fires of hatred. Another social crime that inflamed the Pueblos involved the seizure of Indian orphans, their removal from the village, and their placement in Spanish households where, in theory, they were to be cared for and educated. In actuality, such orphans became servants and were subjected to brutal punishment if they attempted to flee. The Pueblos insisted that they were able to care for their own orphans and that the entire program was a pretext for acquiring cheap labor.

From the foregoing, it should be obvious that the Pueblo people had abundant provocation spurring them on toward revolt. To their good fortune, several other factors figured in the successful outcome of the plot. One was the disunity in Spanish ranks: throughout much of the seventeenth century bitter factionalism divided provincial officials and the Franciscan missionaries. Petty jurisdictional matters were the main source of friction, but the feuding which resulted so distracted the European community that it failed to pay proper heed to the signs of an impending Indian upheaval.

Another circumstance aiding the Pueblos was the Spaniards' state of unpreparedness. New Mexico possessed no regular military garrison, depending for protection instead upon an informal militia composed of all able-bodied men in the province. Most of them lived in scattered farms and ranches, which meant that it was impossible to assemble a defensive force with any celerity. The colonists were so dispersed, according to Father Ayeta, that to call up a troop of as few as thirty men took considerable doing. Because of this, he noted soon after the Revolt, the people had not been able to help each other when hostilities broke forth, and the Indians had swept the country-side almost unopposed. Governor Otermín emphatically agreed, declaring that New Mexico had been lost to the rebels because its settlers lived so far apart they were incapable of mustering effective resistance. That fact, no doubt, had been fully assessed by Popé and

Pueblos gathering for battle.
Museum of New Mexico photograph
neg. no. 20205

other Indian leaders and probably encouraged them in making the final decision in favor of war.

One character trait commonly attributed to colonial Spaniards—fatalism—seems to have added to their vulnerability. A profound belief that whatever happened was the Almighty's will tended to discourage these colonists from making long-range plans for their own defense. With a resignation that was perhaps typical of the times, Alonso García, while grieving over the death of his son in the Revolt, wrote to an acquaintance, "Courage friend! Since it comes from above and God, our Lord, has ordained it so, we must conform to his holy will." Father Ayeta himself went so far as to declare that the Pueblo Revolt had been carried out with "divine permission."

On balance, it can be said that the bloody events of 1680 had their origin in a variety of religious, cultural, social, and economic causes. All of these, however, were accurately combined and reduced to a single overriding cause by Martín Solís de Miranda, the royal attorney in Mexico City, who after examining much of the documentation in 1682, concluded simply, "The many oppressions which [the Indians] receive from the Spaniards have been the chief reason for the rebellion." ⨯⨯⨯

The principal source of information on the Pueblo Revolt is Charles Wilson Hackett, ed., and Charmion Clair Shelby, trans., *Revolt of the Pueblo Indians of New Mexico and Otermín's Attempted Reconquest, 1680–1682* (2 vols., Albuquerque: University of New Mexico Press, 1942). This work contains, in translation, the bulk of the primary documents associated with the event. It also includes, as an introduction, a lengthy and detailed narrative of the Revolt. All the direct quotes in the foregoing article have been taken from this source.

A useful secondary work, incorporating important archival material not included in Hackett and Shelby, is Jack D. Forbes, *Apache, Navajo, and Spaniard* (Norman: University of Oklahoma Press, 1994). A popular overview of the subject is provided in Robert Silverberg, *The Pueblo Revolt* (Lincoln: University of Nebraska Press, 1994). Franklin Folson reconstructs the Indian side of the Revolt in a highly acclaimed juvenile volume, *Indian Uprising on the Rio Grande* (Albuquerque: University of New Mexico Press, 1996). See also, Andrew L. Knaut, *The Pueblo Revolt of 1680* (Norman: University of Oklahoma Press, 1995).

CHAPTER TWO

MISERY AS A FACTOR
IN COLONIAL LIFE

*One of the most difficult tasks involved in the pursuit of history, as
any reader finds, is that of gaining an accurate idea of the way people
in past centuries perceived themselves and their world. We tend to
think that those who came before were much like ourselves, except that
they dressed differently and had quaint customs.*

*In reality, the mind-set of times now long gone bore scant
resemblance to ours, the circumstances of life then imparting, what
must seem to us, entirely unfamiliar patterns and habit of thought.
An inescapable condition of daily living faced by colonial New
Mexicans was an abiding sense of misery that must be taken into
account when assessing their inner life and the impact hardship had
on their personal histories.*

O N SEPTEMBER 8, 1680, Governor Antonio de Otermín wrote a lengthy report concerning the great Pueblo Revolt that had swept across the Kingdom of New Mexico less than a month before. In that catastrophe, twenty-one missionary friars and more than 350 colonists had lost their lives, and Spanish rule north of El Paso had been extinguished.

The governor in his report used a recurring phrase to refer to New Mexico. Repeatedly, he called it, "this miserable kingdom."[1] Those were not new words applied in the aftermath of the bloody revolt, but rather they represented an expression that over the years had become commonplace in dispatches sent to Mexico City by frustrated and desperate officials in Santa Fe.[2] Indeed, both in the centuries before and after the 1680 tragedy crown officers, churchmen, and others regularly used the terms "miserable" and "misery" in speaking of New Mexico's land and people.

Spanish scholar Américo Castro has suggested that misery and misfortune have dogged the people of Spain from the beginnings of their history.[3] That view finds an echo in the writings of numerous other social commentators, as, for example, Ramón Menéndez Pidal who asserts that the Spaniard traditionally has led "a way of life devoid of comforts."[4] Or as William Lytle Schurz put it, "Life is hard for him . . . he has never known what 'security' is . . . for there is little abundance in Spain."[5]

The conditions or circumstances contributing to a state of misery in the Mother Country were evidently duplicated in the colonies, at least in New Spain. At the end of the eighteenth century, Bishop Manuel Abad y Queipo of Michoacán observed that in colonial society there were no "gradations between classes, no middle position. There are only the rich or the miserable, the noble or the vile." In his view the large majority, comprising mixed-bloods and Indians, were in a state of want because of "their color, ignorance, and misery."[6]

A "poverty of possessions"
characterized early New Mexican life.

Another outspoken figure of the late colonial years, Miguel
Ramos de Arizpe, found the chief source of misery in archaic
economic policies imposed by the royal government, rather than in
social inequities. As the elected representative of New Spain's four
Eastern Interior Provinces to the Cortes in Cádiz, he presented in
1811 a report to that body indicting the colonial commercial system,
"which although it has enriched a few, has impoverished and kept all
the rest of the Spaniards wrapped in misery. . . ." When residents of
his province, he noted, attempt to do business at annual trade fairs
they experience firsthand the evil effects of restricted commerce, so
they end by paying "tribute to their miserable bondage." And later,
with a dramatic flourish, he speaks of his people's "tears born of
misery."[7] A half-century afterward, a Mexican observer stated that
the misery had long since become permanent.[8]

Perhaps nowhere in the Spanish Empire can better examples be found of the conditions that reduced colonists to a state of misery than in Governor Otermín's "miserable kingdom" of New Mexico. Although other regions of New Spain's northern frontier suffered through natural and man-made disasters, none seemed quite as awash in misery as benighted New Mexico.

In English, the word misery bears the primary meaning of wretched and the secondary meaning of poverty-stricken. In the Spanish language of colonial New Mexico, however, *miseria* definitely signified poverty, in the first instance. But then, we should note that Hispanic poverty was virtually synonymous with wretchedness of circumstances.

Upon reaching Santa Fe for the first time in 1704, New Mexico Governor Francisco Cuervo y Valdés hastily wrote to the king, declaring his astonishment at seeing so much "want and misery."[9] Being a native of Spain and a well-traveled man, the Governor's words can be given considerable credence. So too can those of Durango's Bishop Benito Crespo who made a personal visit to the upper Rio Grande in 1730. "This land is the poorest I have seen," he reported bleakly.[10]

The poverty of the country—its scarcity of resources—was a recurring theme in contemporary documents. Father García de San Francisco at Senecú below Socorro spoke in 1661 of "this miserable land of New Mexico."[11] And Governor Alberto Maynez in 1815 judged that his jurisdiction "*es país miserable por naturaleza*" (is inherently a miserable country).[12]

It is clear that human misery was a condition of life in New Mexico even before the arrival of the Spaniards. Anthropologists Wittfogel and Goldfrank remind us that, "The nightmare of a world that is dry and barren recurs hauntingly in the Zuni emergence myth as well as in recent stories. Zuni memory is emphatic about the tribe's former poverty and insecurity. . . . It is more than probable that the feeling of insecurity [was] to some extent present in all the Pueblos."[13] Hawley, Pijoan and Elkin, for example, noted in the early 1940s in a study of Zia that, "The possibility of food shortage . . . is the primary anxiety of each individual in the pueblo."[14]

The fact is, conditions of aridity offered only limited opportunities

*Rustic dwellings bespoke the harsh
realities of daily living.*
Museum of New Mexico photograph
neg. no. 37438

*Arid and harsh landscape of New
Mexico contributed to the miseries
heaped upon colonial settlers.*
Museum of New Mexico photograph,
no negative number

in New Mexico for the practice of agriculture. Land suitable for irrigation was not plentiful, and dry-farming was at best small-scale and often no more than marginally successful. Originally, the Pueblos had sought to combat the specter of famine by storing away as much as a seven-years' supply of grain.

When the first Spaniards learned of this custom, they at once imposed levies upon the Indians' horde of corn and the reserves were rapidly depleted. As a result, the drought and ensuing famine of the 1660s took a heavy toll among the Pueblos. A short time before this disaster, a Franciscan missionary had referred to the inhabitants of New Mexico, both Indian and European, as "poor and miserable subjects."[15] Perhaps the wonder is that in the face of famine the colony survived at all.

Periodic drought, accompanied by suffering and death, was accepted in Hispanic New Mexico. Residents of El Paso Valley characterized themselves in 1780 as, "the miserable people who inhabit these remote lands."[16] The governor at Santa Fe sounded a similar note in 1806 when he described the scarcity and misery produced by drought and bad harvests. And he cited the large number of "miserable ones, experiencing hunger" as a consequence of crop failure.[17]

As the population expanded in the later colonial and early Mexican periods, the increasing shortage of available farmland caused almost as much hardship as the regular droughts. In petitioning for farm plots on the Pecos River in 1822, Manuel Antonio Rivera supplied an example. In approaching the appropriate government agency with a request for a grant, he wrote: "I appear before you and inform you of the misery incurred by me and by other individuals with me, as to our wives and children for not having any lands where we could plant some corn."[18]

Clearly, the degree of misery prevailing in New Mexico was most commonly governed by problems of food production. Yet, all areas of economic endeavor here were retarded so that the wretchedness of daily life can properly be said to have had multiple causes. Stock raising was inhibited by unrelenting Indian hostilities. Mining failed to develop through lack of technical knowledge and capital.

Timbering received no encouragement because of poor transportation and the total absence of sawmills. Unimproved roads and trails plus vast distances imposed a serious check on commerce.

The few cottage industries had limited access to markets, and hence, found it impossible to expand. And finally, official manipulation of the coinage and arbitrary government controls over many facets of the economy kept business at all levels in turmoil. Consequently, New Mexicans knew little else than a familiar misery.

In 1806 Governor Joaquin Real Alencaster, assessing the fruits of two centuries of privation and misery, painted a most unflattering picture of New Mexico's citizenry. In an official report, he depicted them as "miserable creatures" with few skills or abilities, unfit for soldiering, and indifferent to the universal misery and ignorance that plagued their frontier society.[19] Later when Anglo-Americans entered the Southwest by way of the Santa Fe Trail and wrote in their journals of the backwardness and misery manifested in all departments of domestic life, they were merely restating an observation that Hispanic commentators had been making for centuries.

The portrait of New Mexico's bleakness presented here can provide a salutary antidote to the romantic gloss that has come to overlay the Spanish colonial years. Nevertheless, care must be taken not to overstate the case. While New Mexico may have, indeed, been isolated, poor, and unprogressive, still its people managed to maintain their hold on the land in the face of unparalleled adversity and even to grow in numbers, so that at the end of the Spanish era theirs was the most populous and important of New Spain's far northern borderland provinces. ◈

CHAPTER THREE

THE FOUNDING OF ALBUQUERQUE: ANOTHER LOOK

The urban tradition in old Spain ran strong and deep, extending back into Roman times. Spanish municipalities enjoyed extraordinary privileges and powers, guaranteed by ancient legal code. Town planning on the traditional model was introduced into the American colonies, and founders were strictly guided by royal ordinances.

New Mexico in the colonial period saw establishment of four chartered towns, starting with the capital of Santa Fe, formally laid out in 1610, and followed in succession by El Paso, Santa Cruz de la Cañada, and Albuquerque. In each case, details surrounding the founding are poorly recorded. However, somewhat more information is available for the beginnings of Albuquerque, allowing the assembly of a fragmentary case study that suggests the general pattern of municipal organization and development, and the sort of problems that might affect the process.

O N April 23, 1706, some seventy years before the American Revolution, Governor Francisco Cuervo y Valdés of New Mexico sat at a writing table in the dimly lit halls of his mud palace on the Santa Fe plaza. He was composing a formal document to his sovereign in Spain and to the viceroy in Mexico City, attesting to the creation of a new town. Deftly he wrote, "I certify to the king, our lord, and to the most excellent señor viceroy . . . That I founded a villa on the banks and in the valley of the Río del Norte in a good place as regards land, water, pasture, and firewood . . . I gave it as patron titular saint the glorious apostle of the Indies, Señor Francisco Xavier, and called and named it the villa of Alburquerque."[1]

With a hint of pride in his words, Governor Cuervo went on to relate the progress that had been made to date. Thirty-five families, he asserted, had already taken up residence in the town, comprising 252 adults and children. A spacious church had been completed, and a house for the priest was well underway. A start had been made on the *casas reales*, that is, the government buildings for local officials. The settlers had finished their houses, which were provided with corrals for livestock. Irrigation ditches were open and running. Crops were sown. The town was now in good order, well-arranged, and all had been achieved without any expense to the Royal Treasury. This last implied that the people themselves had borne the entire costs for the town's founding.

The governor wished to emphasize the legality of his actions. Therefore, he declared that he had followed the procedures prescribed for the establishment of new municipalities as set forth in the royal laws contained in the *Recopilación*, the law book that governed the conduct of colonial officials. Having said that, and having added a note attesting to the refounding of the pueblo of Galisteo, which had been abandoned during the turbulence of the Pueblo Revolt and reconquest, Francisco Cuervo y Valdés affixed his signature to the paper, had it witnessed by his secretary, and sealed it with an impression of his coat of arms.[2]

The governor's words contained in this formal document of certification are straightforward and clear enough: he founded the villa of Albuquerque in 1706, he provided his superiors certain details about the number of settlers and the buildings then under construction or already completed, and he stated that the project had been carried out in strict conformity with the law. The legal code, which he referred to as the *Recopilación*, was the celebrated *Recopilación de Leyes de los Reynos de las Indias*, Spain's monumental compilation of laws covering practically all aspects of colonial government and public life. One section dealt specifically with the procedures and requirements for creation of new towns.

According to that code, a minimum of thirty family heads was necessary to charter a villa. The site chosen should have good water, arable land, and some timber, if possible. The town received four square leagues of land, measured with a cord. At its center, space was to be marked off for a plaza, a church, and government buildings. As soon as streets were laid out, each family should be given a lot for a house and assigned farm plots in severalty. After living upon the lots and improving the farmland for a specified number of years, residents obtained final title. Portions of the town grant, not distributed to citizens, were reserved as commons (*ejidos*) available to all for pasturing, wood gathering, or rock quarrying. Further, a villa was to have an elected council (*cabildo*) with jurisdiction over executive and judicial affairs of the municipality.[3] These major provisions, and other minor ones, were all designed to provide Spanish colonial towns with an orderly form of government.

Three days after certifying to the founding of Albuquerque, Governor Cuervo wrote a letter to the Viceroy, Francisco Fernández de la Cueva, Duke of Alburquerque.[4] In it he provided background information about the new villa that had not been included in the earlier notice of certification. Motivated by a desire to see New Mexico expand and prosper, Governor Cuervo said that he had issued orders for the placing of a villa on the river below Bernalillo and Alameda. In

*Viceroy of New Spain, Duke of
Alburquerque, for whom the
city was named.*
After Rivera Cambas

advance of actual settlement, he had sent one of his subordinates,
General Juan de Ulibarrí, to scout the area and find a suitable site. The
spot Ulibarrí selected possessed the necessary tillable land, water,
pasture, and firewood, as the law required. It had other natural
advantages, too, which though left unmentioned by Cuervo in his
letter to the viceroy, could scarcely have escaped notice. For one, the
center of the proposed villa was situated on ground slightly elevated
above the surrounding bottom lands, affording some protection from
periodic flooding by the Rio Grande, or Río del Norte as the governor
called it. For another, the geographical position of the town appeared
ideal as far as the practical needs of the future settlers were concerned.

It lay astride the Camino Real, a good ford on the river existed nearby to the west, and a dozen miles due eastward yawned the mouth of the Cañon de Carnué (Tijeras Canyon), a pass giving access to the plains beyond the Sandia Mountains.

Once the site had been chosen, Cuervo explained that he made a public announcement throughout the province inviting citizens to join in creating the new community. Many families responded, he told the viceroy, bringing with them herds of cattle and flocks of sheep. For security, he detached a squad of ten soldiers from the Santa Fe presidio and sent it to escort the settlers while on the road and then to take up permanent guard duty at the villa. The troops, accompanied by their families, were led by Captain Martín Hurtado. Their presence played an important part in attracting participants to the endeavor, because, as the governor himself noted gravely, the country south of Bernalillo was alive with hostile Apaches. Even as few as ten soldiers stationed in the villa could offer considerable comfort to the Spanish colonists.

Thus far Governor Cuervo had provided the viceroy with simple information, but now he could not resist the temptation to make an optimistic forecast about his municipal creation. "I do not doubt, very excellent lord, that in a short time this will be the most prosperous Villa for its growth of cattle and abundance of grain, because of its great fertility and for [my] having given it, in spiritual and temporal things, the patron saints that I have chosen, namely the ever glorious apostle of the Indies, San Francisco Xavier, and Your Excellency, with whose names the town has been entitled Villa de Alburquerque de San Francisco Xavier del Bosque."[5] Clearly the governor was bucking for favor when he gave the viceroy's name to the new town.

In conclusion, Cuervo declared, "The Villa was sworn, taking into account the things ordered by his Majesty in his royal laws."[6] By the word "sworn," he meant that the heads of households had taken an oath as charter citizens to live upon and improve lands allotted to them as a requirement for gaining final title of possession.

From the foregoing statements, it is clear Governor Cuervo intended to show that, through his own efforts, he had assembled a respectable number of colonists and chartered the new villa of Albuquerque; that he had ordered delineation of the outer boundaries of the community as well as the marking of a site for a plaza; and that he had caused a church and government offices to be built. Unfortunately, other evidence indicates that the ambitious governor, in his claims, strayed several degrees from the truth. Indeed, as a subsequent review of other documents will show, he uttered numerous half-truths and several outright falsehoods. Some doubt is, therefore, cast upon the traditional belief that Albuquerque was founded as a lawful Spanish municipality.

The subject is of more than academic interest. As child and heir of the Spanish colonial villa, the modern city of Albuquerque has on occasion asserted claim to land and water rights in the courts by reference to Hispanic law governing the community at its founding. Such a stand has always been predicated upon the position that Governor Cuervo, true to his word to the king and viceroy, conducted the formal proceedings and followed the steps as stipulated by the *Recopilación* that were needed to establish Albuquerque as a legal entity.

In 1881, at the beginning of the boom occasioned by arrival of the railroad, the city of Albuquerque placed a petition before the state Surveyor General asking that he survey a tract of four square leagues (roughly 17.2 square miles), centering upon the Old Town plaza, and then recommend to Congress that it place Albuquerque in possession. The claim was based solely upon the old Spanish practice of granting four square leagues to each new villa. Although Governor Cuervo had never referred in existing documents to such a grant, it has always been supposed that one was made, owing to his sweeping assertion that he had hewed to the letter of the law as spelled out in the *Recopilación*.

The Surveyor General of New Mexico evidently assumed as much, for he acted favorably upon Albuquerque's petition, surveyed the "imagined" four square leagues, and recommended it for confirmation by Congress. He was careful to explain to Washington, however, that, "No original documents constituting or creating the grant hereby are

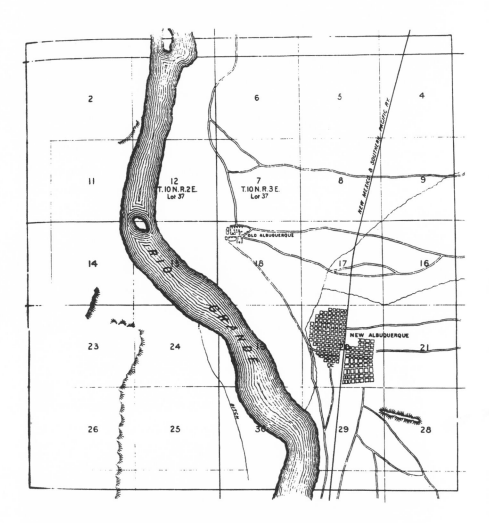

TOWN OF ALBUQUERQUE GRANT. NO. 130.

SCALE 50 CHAINS = 1 INCH.　AREA 17361.06 ACRES.

The field notes of the survey of Private Land Claim No. 130 the Town of Albuquerque Grant, from which this plat has been made have been examined and approved and are on file in this office.
U.S. Surveyor General's Office
Santa Fé, New Mexico,
November 28, 1883.

Henry W. Atkinson

U.S. Surveyor General

1883 survey map of the Town of Albuquerque showing Old Town's location, which was unchanged from the eighteenth century.

known to exist, and therefore no such document can be filed herewith."[7] What he supposed, as have most lawyers and historians since, was that the original grant papers, which Cuervo must have drawn up, had become lost over the years, but that unfortunate circumstance notwithstanding, Albuquerque was still entitled to its four leagues of land. The tough-minded Congressmen, though, were not swayed by such an argument, and eventually the city's claim was disallowed.

The issue came up again in 1959, but this time in relation to water rights. The city became involved in a dispute with the state over use of waters in the surrounding Rio Grande basin. It claimed that under Spanish law the villa of Albuquerque was conceded all the water necessary for its growth and development and that since the modern city was the legal heir of the villa, its right in this regard remained unimpaired. The New Mexico Supreme Court finally decided against the city on the basis of other legal points. Yet what is significant here is that much of Albuquerque's stand rested upon the popular assumption that in the year 1706 Governor Francisco Cuervo y Valdés officially established a valid community according to the laws of Spain.[8]

It is now possible to clarify, in some measure, the incidents attendant upon Albuquerque's beginnings, particularly the actions of Governor Cuervo. But since serious gaps still exist in the documentary record, our picture, though revised and brought into sharper focus, remains disappointingly fuzzy around the edges. Keeping that fact in mind, we can begin by taking a close look at what was going on in New Mexico, and especially in the Middle Rio Grande Valley, during the years immediately prior to 1706.

When Governor Diego de Vargas died at Bernalillo in April 1704, his second in command Juan Paéz Hurtado, a native of Andalucia and a staunch soldier, took charge of the province. At once he notified the viceroy, the Duke of Alburquerque, of Vargas's passing, and then he set about holding things together until a replacement could be named.

Paéz Hurtado had no easy task, for New Mexico was in a state of extraordinary disarray. Predatory bands of Apache and Navajo stalked the small Spanish settlements and ranches, and nothing the few score soldiers were able to do seemed to stem their constant attacks. Those same soldiers, in whose hands defense of the frontier lay, suffered from lack of provisions, a shortage of horses, inadequate pay, and low morale. Compounding the Indian problem, some of the western Pueblos still refused to submit to Spanish rule. The Zuni, after first pledging loyalty, had changed their minds and abandoning their pueblo fled to a neighboring mesa top where they remained until a Spanish priest talked them down in 1705. The Hopi, still farther west, continued defiant and, indeed, would persist as a thorn in the side of Spanish governors throughout the remainder of the colonial period.

The settler folk who had come with Vargas in 1693 and others who arrived in a thin but steady trickle in succeeding years had not fared well. Government support in the form of provisions and tools sustained them initially, while they commenced to rebuild the province, but such aid was drastically curtailed in 1698 when officials of the royal treasury in Mexico City arbitrarily decided that New Mexicans should have made enough headway by then to go it alone. The loss of material backing unluckily coincided with the beginning of a severe drought that stretched without relief from 1698 to 1704. Streams evaporated, scorched pastureland was grazed over and became ankle-deep in dust. Crops withered and produced at harvest scarcely enough seed for the next planting. Livestock wasted away. And hunger became a grim spectre stalking the colonists. The stars, it seemed, were aligned against them.[9]

The miserable economic conditions led inevitably to social discord. Petty controversies split the populace into squabbling factions and produced so much poisoned air that many embittered persons threatened to pull stakes and return to El Paso.

It was this atmosphere of despair and gloom that Francisco Cuervo y Valdés found when he arrived at Santa Fe on March 10, 1705, to take over the reins of government. He had received his appointment to office directly from the viceroy, on condition that the king approve. But since such approval might be months in coming, owing to the slowness of trans-Atlantic mail service, Cuervo had hastened on to New Mexico to begin at once putting affairs there in order. Until confirmed in office, he would be merely the provisional governor. That temporary status perhaps explains his strenuous efforts to make a good showing during the first months after his arrival.[10]

Cuervo was well fitted by background and experience to follow in the footsteps of the lamented Governor Vargas. A native of Santa María de Grado in the province of Asturias, northern Spain, his family was evidently of the nobility, for noble lineage was one of the requirements for membership in the military order of Santiago, to which Cuervo was elected sometime after 1698.[11]

He arrived in the New World in the year 1678 and proceeded to Sonora (which included much of present-day southern Arizona) where he took up duties as an infantry captain. Three years later, he became lieutenant governor of the province. Thereafter, he served in succession as the military governor of the provinces of Nuevo Léon and Coahuila, which lay immediately to the south of Texas. It was his skillful performance in the handling of those offices and his wide knowledge of frontier affairs that led the Duke of Alburquerque to name him to the governorship of New Mexico late in 1704.

Once in Santa Fe, Cuervo made a hasty survey of local conditions and discovered excellent grounds for apprehension. The depth of his dismay is evident in words he addressed to the king. "I have never seen so much want, misery, and backwardness in my life," he wrote His Majesty. "I suspect this land was better off before the Spaniards came."[12] Such a candid admission indicates that the new governor was something of a realist.

Since military defense was one of his prime concerns, Cuervo undertook a quick inspection of the one hundred regular troops attached to the Santa Fe presidio. Then he called for a general muster of the citizens' militia. Because of the constant danger from hostile Indians, all able-bodied men were enrolled in militia companies. Under orders of the governor, those from the towns of Santa Cruz de la Cañada and Bernalillo marched to the capital for a review and inspection. The Bernalillo contingent, the military records note, was led by three captains: Fernando de Chávez, Diego de Montoya, and Manuel Baca. All were destined to play a prominent role in the early history of Albuquerque.[13]

With a coldly professional eye, Governor Cuervo tallied up his forces, both regular and volunteer, and determined that their number was far too small to defend his broad domain. He fired off a letter to Mexico City asking for reinforcements, but as he may well have anticipated, the economy-minded viceroy simply pigeonholed the request. No more soldiers were to be forthcoming.

The governor's next move was to take the troops already quartered in Santa Fe and spread them out on the frontier. He hoped that by patrolling the danger zones with small squads, the Apaches and other tribes could be stopped from running roughshod over the New Mexican settlements. To that end, temporary detachments were stationed at the pueblos of Santa Clara, Cochiti, Jemez, Laguna, Acoma, and Zuni.

As part of a broad policy to gain cooperation of the Pueblo Indians, Cuervo toured their villages, spoke to the leaders in conciliatory terms, and obtained promises of aid in the continuing war against the Apache. From these meetings, he drew a high opinion of the Pueblo people, referring to them as handsome in appearance and industrious by nature.[14] The Indians, for their part, responded favorably to the governor's overtures. Indeed, they came to regard him as something of a savior, or so he tried to convince the king. By letter, Cuervo declared immodestly that Pueblo spokesmen who gathered at Santa Fe in January 1706 voluntarily composed a document urging that "Don Francisco Cuervo y Valdés be continued and maintained in this administration for such time as is His Majesty's will . . ."[15]

The implication is plain. Worried over his pending confirmation, the governor had contrived an endorsement from the Indians in a bid to polish his image and win approval from the crown. Something of the same motive, in part, was behind Cuervo's move to create a new villa in the Bosque de Doña Luisa. Certainly, he exaggerated on paper the dimensions of the project and his role in its initiation, as we shall see shortly.

Actually, interest in founding a villa somewhere in the Middle Valley of the Rio Grande had existed long before Cuervo y Valdés assumed the governorship. The idea first surfaced in 1662 when Governor Peñalosa made an unsuccessful attempt to promote a town in that area. The matter came up again after the revolt and reconquest. The municipal council of Santa Fe in 1698 called upon the governor to establish a villa in the Río Abajo, but once more, nothing was done.[16]

While officialdom may have been guilty of heel dragging with regard to organizing a formal villa, the same could not be said for individual Spanish colonists who were eager to develop the potentially rich agricultural lands of the Middle Valley. Some of them had peeled off from Vargas's returning column in 1693 and reoccupied portions of the valley, especially the Bernalillo district. Over the next several years, Governor Vargas made a number of land grants to persons who desired farms in the country between Alameda and the swamps of Mejía. One of those grants, issued in the summer of 1704, went to Luís García, who reclaimed the estate of his grandfather, the former lieutenant governor, Alonso García.[17]

The pueblo of Alameda itself, which had been burned by the Spaniards in the aftermath of the Pueblo Revolt, remained untenanted until 1702 when missionaries gathered about fifty stray Tiwas and rebuilt the village. This population, however, was evidently too small to maintain a viable community, and six years later the Indians moved downstream and joined Isleta Pueblo.[18] That left the abundant and fertile farmland, stretching south from Bernalillo, available to Spanish citizens who might wish to apply for grants.

One nucleus of settlement, predating the founding of Albuquerque, was the village of Atrisco, located on the west bank of the river and facing the site of the future villa. At least by 1703, the place was recognized as a community even though in form it was no more than a collection of farms. Lacking any municipal organization, Atrisco was attached for administrative purposes first to Bernalillo and then, after 1706, to Albuquerque. Throughout the remainder of the colonial period, the village was a satellite of its larger neighbor, and in fact was often spoke of as "Atrisco de Albuquerque."[19]

One thing is clear then: a number of Spanish property holdings existed on both sides of the Rio Grande well before Governor Cuervo certified to the king and viceroy in the spring of 1706 that he had founded the Villa of Albuquerque. But in spite of that start, there had been no great rush of settlers from elsewhere in New Mexico to claim a share of the plentiful cropland and pasture available in the region. The vulnerability of the valley to Indian attack offered the major stumbling block to expansion of settlement. That problem, Cuervo hoped to alleviate by stationing a detachment of ten soldiers at the new villa. Their presence plainly proved to be a key factor in luring colonists to Albuquerque.

Information surrounding the actual formation of the villa, including the ceremonial taking of possession and distribution of lands to residents, is very thin. Most writers have tried to reconstruct a picture of the event by reference to procedures set down in Spanish law and to ceremonies, described at a later date, for the founding of New Mexico towns.[20] There would seem to be justification for such guessing because Governor Cuervo, as noted, did give the king flat assurance that in establishing Albuquerque he followed the laws as set down in the *Recopilación*.

In a remote area such as New Mexico, however, some flexibility in application of the laws seems to have been permitted. Governor Vargas, for example, upon creating the villa of Santa Cruz in 1695, placed it under an appointed alcalde mayor, who also had the title of militia captain, rather than under the usual elective municipal council, or cabildo. As he pointed out, he gave the town "this style and form of government because of its being on the frontier."[21] In addition, he specifically decreed that Santa Fe, the first villa of the province, should alone have the privilege of operating under a municipal council. The precedent established by that order as well as Albuquerque's status as a frontier community, perhaps explain why Governor Cuervo in chartering his new villa in 1706 provided it with an alcalde mayor rather than a cabildo.

A native-born New Mexican, forty-six-year-old Captain Martín Hurtado was the man Governor Cuervo selected to serve as the first alcalde mayor of the Villa of Alburquerque, as well as the commander of the ten-man military squad to be garrisoned there. To Hurtado must go credit for partitioning lands among charter members of the villa, which he did during January 1706, and for conducting the founding ceremony on the following February 7. We would like to believe that the assembled populace gathered at the spot selected for a plaza, participated in the marking off of streets and town lots, and helped designate the sites for a church and soldiers' quarters. They would also have followed behind Captain Hurtado while the town's lawful four square leagues were measured and marked. In conformity with ancient Spanish custom, they would have pulled up grass, thrown rocks in the air, and shouted, "long live the king," symbolic acts associated with the taking possession of new lands. Later, some of the colonists recorded that they had sworn on oath, which confirms that some kind of formal proceedings took place. But whether the four leagues were actually surveyed and whether plaza, streets, lots, and commons were marked is open to question.[22]

Further uncertainty surrounds the actual number of charter citizens. The governor's own declaration that there were thirty-five families with 252 people has generally been accepted by scholars. But Juan Candelaria, recollecting seventy years after the fact, stated that the villa got its start when twelve families from Bernalillo moved to the site, accompanied by the soldier escort that Governor Cuervo had assigned to them.[23]

A wholly different picture emerges from the records of an investigation into the governor's activities that was conducted in 1712, after he had left office and returned to Mexico. At that time the king's ministers, while reviewing documents in their archive, discovered discrepancies in some of the claims put forth by former governor Cuervo y Valdés of New Mexico. As a result, they prevailed upon the crown to issue a royal *cédula*, or decree, directing the current governor of the province, Juan Ignacio Flores Mogollon, to open an official inquiry. Specifically, they wanted to know whether Albuquerque had been legally founded and whether the charter families had numbered thirty-five, as Cuervo maintained. They also asked that his claims to having created another villa north of Santa Fe, called Santa María de Grado, and having refounded the abandoned pueblos of Galisteo and Pojoaque with displaced Indians be examined.

At Santa Fe, Governor Flores Mogollon, upon receiving the king's cédula, appointed Vargas's old friend and subordinate, General Juan Paéz Hurtado, to carry out the investigation. The general spent several months traveling about the province taking depositions from citizens, and his findings, particularly as they relate to the beginnings of Albuquerque, are most illuminating.

Opening the judicial inquiry at the Villa of Albuquerque on October 21, 1712, Paéz Hurtado summoned witnesses and received their testimony "under the sign of the cross," that is, under oath. Here is the statement of Pedro Azencio López:

QUESTION: Was he one of the founding citizens of the villa which was settled by order of Don Francisco Cuervo?

LÓPEZ: That was true. He had joined with his father, Pedro López, when the governor founded it.

QUESTION: How many persons were in his family?

LÓPEZ: Five.

QUESTION: Did he know the total number of founding families?

LÓPEZ: There were nineteen original families, plus the ten soldiers, with their women and children, who served as guard for the vicinity. The nineteen families at the time comprised 103 people, not counting dependents of the soldiers. Now they totaled 129 people.

QUESTION: Had the said Don Francisco Cuervo provided them any government aid (*ayuda de costa*) at the founding?

LÓPEZ: He knew of none.

QUESTION: Had the villa been established in proper form with streets and a plaza?

LÓPEZ: He and the other settlers had moved into the houses abandoned by the Spaniards in 1680, occupying the same estancias and farms. What was called the villa stretched for more than two and a half miles (one league) from the first house to the last.

Plaza of Albuquerque, 1856.
Museum of New Mexico photograph
neg. no. 71389

QUESTION: Were there now any families here beyond those settled
by Don Francisco Cuervo?

LÓPEZ: Yes. Seven additional families with twenty-two people.

Pedro López then declared that he knew no more about the
matter and was dismissed. A succession of other witnesses gave similar
testimony, in each case verifying López's population figures. From
their statements, a few supplementary details can be gleaned. For
example, Captain Fernando Durán y Chávez, long one of the leading
men of the valley, was asked if Albuquerque had been lawfully formed
with streets and a plaza, as His Majesty required. He responded that
from the day of its founding, the villa had the same layout as it did

then, with the residents living in homes built before 1680. They were scattered for a league from the first house of Baltasar Romero on the north [at modern Ranchos de Albuquerque] to the last house on the south, that of Pedro López [below Central Avenue]. All of this area, he noted, was heavily wooded (*en mucha alameda*). And, he reports that it was by the authority of Governor Cuervo that the pre-revolt estancias and farms were allotted to the new citizenry.

From these declarations, it can be seen that the governor's original account to the king and viceroy in 1706 varied rather widely from that of the witnesses interviewed by General Paéz Hurtado. Not only that, the general learned in his continuing investigation that Cuervo had fraudulently claimed to have created a new villa above Santa Fe, naming it after his birthplace in Spain, Santa María de Grado. No such town, in fact, had been founded. Further, while the governor had actually resettled the pueblos of Galisteo and Pojoaque in the north, he grossly inflated the number of Indians involved. All this Paéz Hurtado entered into the formal record of his inquiry.[24]

As already indicated, Governor Cuervo y Valdés seemed to have been intent upon currying favor among his superiors. No doubt, it was that simple motive which led him to color the truth. To the Spanish mind, the founding of a villa carried immense prestige, and the governor beyond question wished to add that accolade to his name. An eighteenth-century friar-scholar, Silvestre Vélez de Escalante, who composed a history of early New Mexico, wrote with biting sarcasm that Governor Cuervo, "eager to accumulate merits, falsified his reports."[25] It is difficult to disagree with that judgment.

But where does that leave us with regard to the status and early history of Albuquerque? Must all of Cuervo's utterances on its founding be dismissed, or did he mix truth with fiction? Is it possible to draw any satisfactory conclusions on the matter at this late date?

Assimilating all currently available information, this much seems evident. Governor Cuervo, in writing to his superiors, portrayed himself as the architect of the new and glorious villa of Albuquerque. He erroneously claimed a founding population of thirty-five families, when in fact there were little more than half that number. Perhaps the governor pumped up the figure so that it would surpass, by a comfortable margin, the minimum requirement of thirty families as specified in *Recopilación*. Very few of the other stipulations pertaining to new villas seem to have been met. Whatever was done, must have been performed in the most casual, haphazard manner. At the time of the judicial inquiry of 1712, none of the witnesses indicated that even the elementary task of designating a plaza and streets had been carried out. Nor did they make reference to the building of a church, although other contemporary documents affirm that one was in progress during the villa's first years. Certainly, Governor Cuervo's solemn assertion to the king in 1706 that a church was already completed must be viewed with skepticism.

What appears to have occurred is this: Upon learning that ten soldiers were to be stationed in the area, nineteen families migrated to the Albuquerque valley, probably coming in piecemeal fashion, that is, not in a body, and, upon arrival they were assigned individual land grants. Many of those, especially the twelve families Juan Candelaria mentions as coming from Bernalillo, were actually reclaiming properties that had belonged to their ancestors before the revolt of 1680. All households, so far as we can tell, received private grants of farm and ranch land. There is no evidence that any family was enrolled as a member of the four-square-league community grant alleged to have been made to the Villa of Alburquerque. As the settlers in 1712 made plain, Albuquerque was not the usual compact urban town one thought of in connection with the rank and title of a villa. Rather it was a mere collection of farms spread along the Rio Grande. From all reports, this pattern of dispersal continued throughout much of the century.

General Pedro de Rivera, for instance, while on a military inspection tour of New Mexico in 1726, passed through Albuquerque and observed that the majority of its population, made up of Spaniards, mestizos and mulattos, lived on scattered farms. In 1754, Father Manuel Trigo, traveling upriver from Isleta spoke of reaching the villa, "or I might say the site of the villa of Albuquerque, for the settlers, who inhabit it on Sunday, do not live there. They must stay on their farms to keep watch over their cornfields, which are planted at a very pretty place three leagues distant, called La Alameda." And finally as late as 1776, another priest, Fray Francisco Domínguez, spoke of the villa itself as consisting of only twenty-four houses located near the mission. "The rest of what is called Albuquerque," he wrote, "extends upstream to the north, and all of it is a settlement of farms on the meadows of the said river for the distance of a league."[26] It bears mentioning that throughout the colonial years, New Mexico's other villas, Santa Fe and El Paso del Norte, and especially Santa Cruz de la Cañada, all showed similar characteristics of population dispersal and lack of genuine urbanism.

After a church was up and functioning, the Albuquerque citizenry evidently erected second homes, or "Sunday residences," on or near today's Old Town Plaza. Thereafter, for at least the first three-quarters of the eighteenth century, the community retained this loose and informal aspect. Only gradually in later years did a body of permanent residents take root around an emerging plaza. But notwithstanding its uncharacteristic and extra-legal design, the town was known from 1706 onward as the Villa de Alburquerque, and no one appears to have challenged its right to use the prestigious title of "villa." ◈

Sy MM A,
Y RECOPILACION
DE CHIRVGIA, CON VN
Arte para sagrar muy vtil y prouechosa.

COMPVESTA POR MAES-
tre Alonso Lopez, natural de los Inojosos.
Chirujano y enfermero del Ospital de
S. Ioseph de los Yndios, desta muy
insigne Ciudad de Mexico.

DIRIGIDO AL ILL. Y R.
S. Don P. Moya de Contreras, Arçobispo
de Mexico y ael cõcejo de su Magest.

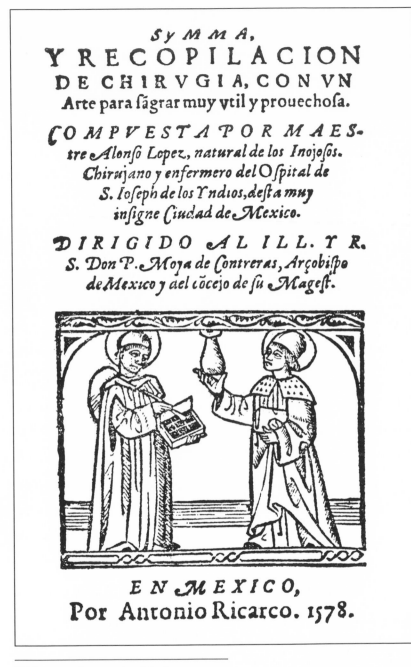

E N MEXICO,
Por Antonio Ricarco. 1578.

---

*Title page of a standard book on surgery
and the practice of bleeding that may
have been brought to New Mexico by
the Oñate expedition in 1598.*

CHAPTER FOUR

COLONIAL PHYSICIANS

The practice of medicine in seventeenth- and eighteenth-century New Mexico was primitive in character, at least by modern standards. The small number of medical personnel, almost all of whom had meager qualifications, confronted epidemics, cases of trauma, malnutrition, parasitosis (intestinal parasites), and occasional instances of poisoning. Here as in Spain, medical treatment was more closely allied to theology than science. Its story in early New Mexico, long neglected, presents abundant opportunities for understanding of the stresses besetting frontier society.

M EDICAL CARE within much of the Spanish Empire was likely to be uncertain at best. Professionally trained doctors could be found in the cities, but elsewhere people often depended on lay healers or simply some older family member, both categories having learned the medical arts through experience reinforced by folk teachings. New Mexico, one of the most isolated colonies, offers a picture of the problems met in delivering basic health care under Spain.

In 1802 the New Mexican governor Fernando de Chacón petitioned to be relieved from office, on grounds that he had suffered physical injuries while traveling on the Camino Real and no medical facilities existed in his province.[1] Five years later, U.S. Army Lieutenant Zebulon M. Pike strayed into Spanish territory and was arrested. Taken first to Santa Fe and then to Chihuahua City, he remarked in his journal on "the deplorable state of the medical sciences in [these] provinces."[2] Such statements, recorded not long before independence, would seem to indicate that little can be said about the early practice of medicine in New Mexico.

A close examination of the documentary record, however, reveals the presence of physicians, surgeons, and other health-care workers who from time to time brought their skills to the Hispanic and Indian peoples living on the upper Rio Grande del Norte. Unfortunately, such practitioners are usually mentioned only in passing, and aside from occasional anecdotal material, we are left largely in the dark with regard to their methods and performance.

The first physician of record to visit the area was a certain Dr. Ramos, who accompanied the exploratory expedition of Francisco Vásquez de Coronado, 1540–1542. After fights with the Pueblo Indians he dressed arrow wounds, and he also ministered to Coronado when he suffered a severe fall from his horse.[3] Juan de Oñate's colonizing expedition of 1598, strangely, had no doctor in its ranks. But one of its officers, Captain Gaspar Pérez de Villagrá, wrote that among the men, there "are expert surgeons [who] treat the wounds of their comrades most skillfully."[4]

Villagrá meant that some of the soldiers were lay surgeons, their knowledge having been acquired through independent study or association with professional surgeons, or even barbers who specialized in the practice. At this date, surgery was primarily limited to amputation, lancing of abscesses, repair of bone fractures, cautery (closing of wounds with a hot iron), and occasional Cesarean operations, permitted by the Church only to save the life of a child upon the death of the mother. The single member of the Oñate expedition who can be identified as one of Villagrá's "surgeons" is the affluent officer Juan del Caso Baraona.

According to a manifest of the inspection conducted before departure, Caso took to New Mexico as part of his equipment and personal belongings, the following:

FIVE POUNDS OF MEDICAMENTS BY RECOGNIZED MASTERS
  [OF PHARMACY?]

TWO CASES OF INSTRUMENTS FOR BLOODLETTING AND DRAINING

SOME SURGICAL INSTRUMENTS

ONE SYRINGE AND FOUR CUPPING GLASSES

TWO POUNDS OF ALUM AND A SMALL AMOUNT OF LEFTOVER
  PHARMACEUTICAL MEDICAMENTS

This list establishes that Juan del Caso, in addition to practicing surgery, was also a bleeder (*sangrador*) and perhaps a pharmacist (*boticario*) as well. Curiously, the inspection report also shows him in possession of a large number of smithing tools, so this versatile man was probably a blacksmith, too.[5] The same report includes an extensive listing of the expedition's general medical supplies, worth 500 pesos and ranging from laxative tablets to mercury ointment for syphilis and four boxes of lancets, the principal instrument used in treating penetrating battle wounds.[6]

Another contemporary document reveals that Juan del Caso owned "cinco libros de medicinas de graves autores."[7] Regrettably, no titles are given, but in all likelihood one would have been Alonso

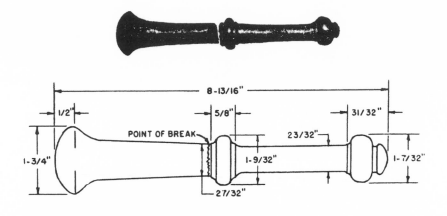

Spanish apothecary pestle (found broken at the center) from the ruins of Tonque Pueblo, eight miles east of San Felipe Pueblo.
Courtesy of Albuquerque Archeological Society

López de Hinojosos's standard *Suma y Recopilación de Cirugía con un arte para sangrar muy útil y provechosa* (1578). Issued at Mexico City, it was the second medical book to be published in the Western Hemisphere. A second edition appeared in 1595, just as Juan de Oñate was formulating plans for his New Mexican colony.[8] Caso's little collection of books by important authors was perhaps the first "medical library" on United States soil.

After the founding of New Mexico, Governor Oñate requested additional missionaries to aid in converting the large numbers of Pueblo Indians. In response, the Franciscan Order sent him six priests and two lay brothers, the little band arriving at the Villa of San Gabriel, New Mexico's new capital, in December of 1600. One of the lay brothers was Fray Damián Escudero, identified as a physician. While his services were most welcome, his tenure proved brief. During the autumn of 1601, when Oñate was away, a large number of disaffected settlers abandoned his government and fled south. Six of the Franciscans, including Dr. Escudero, chose to leave with the deserters.[9]

Sixteenth-century Spanish missionaries viewed themselves as doctors of the soul, but the powerful Franciscan Order also accepted the obligation of ministering to the mortal body. In the first decades after the conquest of Mexico, virtually all teaching of medicine remained in the hands of Franciscan friars. They also opened hospitals, one of them being for Indians, the famous Hospital Real de San José de los Naturales (1530).[10] The headquarters of the Order, the Convento Grande in Mexico City, contained a large and well-stocked pharmacy, which throughout the colonial period supplied distant frontier missions with compounded botanical and chemical remedies to treat a wide variety of diseases.[11] Moreover, missionaries in the field were routinely furnished with surgical instruments, bandages, and, upon request, medical books. When funds and personnel allowed, the Franciscans attempted to establish an infirmary in each mission chapter.

The infirmary in New Mexico was placed at the Keres Pueblo of San Felipe, on a mesa overlooking the Rio Grande some twelve leagues south of the new capital of Santa Fe. Housed in the *convento*, or priests' quarters, the facility was operational by the early 1620s. Fray Cristóbal de Quirós became guardian, or head of the mission about 1621, but the infirmary was in the care of a Franciscan lay brother, Fray Gerónimo de Pedraza, who in 1618 had accompanied the replacement governor Don Juan de Eulate to New Mexico.[12]

Fray Agustín de Vetancurt in his celebrated *Teatro Mexicano*, published in 1697, states that Pedraza was both a boticario and a *cirujano*.[13] Since the royal treasury paid missionaries' salaries, and Spanish law was strict in the matter, it can be assumed that he was properly certified in both capacities.[14] A *protomédico*, or medical examiner, appointed by the cabildo of Mexico City in 1584, licensed physicians, surgeons, and pharmacists and regularly inspected apothecary shops.[15]

Pedraza undoubtedly received his medical training from fellow Franciscans, although by his day Mexico's Royal and Pontifical University (founded 1553) included a school of medicine. However, it gave marginal attention to the teaching of surgery, owing to the lingering medieval prejudice against using a knife on the body. Surgical education in New Spain did not come into its own until opening of

*The outer precincts of San Felipe
Pueblo in 1846, as the American
Army of Conquest marched by. At
the top of the mesa (left) can be seen
the ruins of the seventeenth-century
mission and pueblo, site of the
infirmary.*

the Royal College of Surgery in 1770, which was modeled on Spain's Real Colegio de Cirugía de Cádiz, itself not founded until 1748.[16] Druggists acquired their skills, not in academic schools, but through their guild, although a Franciscan lay brother like Fray Gerónimo de Pedraza might well have received his accreditation as a boticario through an apprenticeship in the pharmacy of the Convento Grande.[17]

The infirmary in San Felipe Pueblo was centrally located, a short distance downriver from the ecclesiastical capital at Santo Domingo Pueblo, making it accessible to the scattered missions in the province. The site was considered to have a particularly healthy climate. All ill or injured missionaries were sent there for treatment and recuperation.[18]

Fray Alonso de Benavides, director of the Order in New Mexico, described Pedraza as "a fine surgeon who in his great charity healed all the sick in the land."[19] Thus the medical services of the infirmary were available to the public at large, Indians as well as Spaniards. Whether the doctor had the help of a *practicante* (surgeon's assistant) and nurses has not come to light.

Benavides related an incident in which Fray Gerónimo treated a pagan Apache chief named Quinía. In a fight, the Indian leader had been shot with an arrow. The flint head remained in the wound, which became infected and filled with pus. Pedraza wished to surgically remove the arrowhead, but the patient refused his consent. So as an alternative, the doctor took a large copper medal containing an image of St. Francis and tied it so tightly over the wound that it penetrated the flesh. On the next day when the medal was removed, the flint stuck to it and the pus freely drained, shortly producing a cure. Chief Quinía was so impressed that he submitted to baptism and became a Christian.[20]

Pedraza died at the convento of San Felipe on May 5, 1664 (probably in his mid seventies) and was buried there.[21] No evidence is known that would prove the infirmary survived his passing. But if it did, it was certainly extinguished at the time of the great Pueblo Revolt of 1680.

As New Mexico experienced population growth and economic development in the eighteenth century, its deficiencies in the delivery of health care became all the more glaring. Only rarely did communities have access to a trained physician, so the slack had to be taken up by folk healers (*curanderas*) and midwives (*parteras*), or even by lay persons who in an emergency struggled to treat trauma cases or provide relief during an epidemic.

Fray Gerónimo de Pedraza's little infirmary must have been sorely missed, for in the second half of the colonial period patients needing professional hospitalization had to seek it outside the province, or else do without. Fray Josef Carral, for example, fell seriously ill in 1788 and sought permission to leave New Mexico to obtain medical attention.[22] Fray Antonio Caballero, priest for Santo Domingo and Cochiti pueblos in 1815, however, upon suffering a badly gangrened leg remained at his post and recovered, evidently with the aid of native practitioners.[23]

Following are the physicians, of whatever category, that can be identified as serving in New Mexico from the 1690s to independence in 1821. Not only are they few in number, but their terms of activity only occasionally overlapped, so that there were years when the province had no doctor at all in residence.

Juan de Ulibarrí, a native of San Luís Potosí, came to New Mexico in 1694 in the wake of the reconquest that closed the Pueblo Revolt era. He is best remembered for heading a military expedition to the Great Plains in 1706, at which time he held the rank of *sargento-mayor*. But he was also referred to as a *cirujano-mayor* (chief surgeon). In that office (1697), he certified as to the physical incapacity of presidial Captain Félix Martínez and recommended that he be allowed to go south for medical treatment.[24] Where Ulibarrí was trained and how much of his time he may have devoted to the practice of medicine are unknown.

A contemporary of his was Antonio Durán de Armijo of Zacatecas who married at Santa Fe in 1695 and listed his occupation as barber. Fray Angélico Chávez states that Durán de Armijo was "a literate man and versed in medicine who appears in many documents as a notary or a physician, being known as 'el Maestro Barbero.'"[25]

The term "barber" had become almost synonymous with "medic"

and was closely identified with the universal practice of bleeding, or phlebotomy. Lancets and fleams were used to open a vein, although when Captain Francisco Chamuscado fell seriously ill in 1582 on the trail out of New Mexico, his men having neither of those instruments bled him using a sharp horseshoe nail.[26] Father Benavides in 1624 imported thirteen lancets for use in the New Mexican missions, plus thirteen copper cuppings and seven others of glass.[27] Cupping, an adjunct of phlebotomy, involved heating a cup to create a vacuum and applying it to the skin to draw blood to the surface.

In that era, almost any serious condition prompted a call for the services of a barber-bleeder, even symptoms arising from internal parasites or acute nutritional deficiencies, both being prevalent among colonial settlers. A 1719 diary kept by New Mexico Governor Antonio de Valverde of a campaign against the Ute and Comanche Indians mentions that some of his men came in contact with poison ivy and were stricken with severe swelling. He "ordered Antonio Durán [de] Armijo, a barber by trade who had knowledge of blood letting, to attend and assist them."[28]

A third health care provider on hand in the 1690s was the Franciscan lay brother Fray Joseph Narváez, stationed at the Villa of Santa Fe, who attended the sick as apothecary and surgeon. He had been summoned to the province by former governor Don Diego de Vargas, but remained only until 1697 when he returned to Mexico City.[29]

The most interesting medical figure of this period was Francisco Xavier Romero, a native of Mexico City who reached New Mexico in 1693 and settled in the Santa Cruz Valley north of Santa Fe where he was listed as both shoemaker and physician. In 1715 he was convicted of killing a Pojoaque Indian's ox and condemned to two years' exile at El Paso. But on being escorted there, he escaped and took sanctuary in the church at the Villa of Albuquerque. Local citizens promptly petitioned Gov. Flores Mogollón to allow Romero "to exercise his trade of surgery" in their town, which had no surgeon or even a barber. The governor complied, changing the place of exile from El Paso to Albuquerque, and ordering Romero to treat the sick without pay.[30]

In their petition, the citizens noted that Romero had been certified and licensed by Flores Mogollón's predecessors to practice surgery. In fact, a newly available collection of Romero's personal papers contains eleven documents relating to his re-certification by successive governors between 1705 and 1744, the year prior to his death. Further, there is a permit of 1731 issued by the alcalde of Albuquerque allowing Romero to practice medicine in that municipal jurisdiction. The governor and alcaldes of New Mexico, therefore, assumed the regulatory functions toward physicians that elsewhere were handled by protomédicos and cabildos.[31]

In 1740 a small party of French Canadians from the Illinois country arrived in New Mexico, hoping to open trade. When they departed, two of their number remained in Santa Fe, and one of those, Jean Baptiste Alarie (Hispanicized as Juan Bautista Alarí, later Alarid) began to practice his trade as a barber and surgeon.[32] By that date, Ulibarrí had died, while Durán de Armijo, in his late sixties, had either retired or was on the verge of retirement. Alarí lived until 1772 and during much of those three decades may have been the only medical man in New Mexico.

Army surgeon Dr. Cristóbal María Larrañaga was attached to the Santa Fe presidio for more than twenty-five years, caring for both soldiers and civilians. The earliest known document placing him in the capital is dated 1785, and he left his practice about 1811.[33] The only other practitioner of record in that era was a barber living at Albuquerque, Vicente Domingues, whom the 1790 census reported to be a native of Nueva Vizcaya.[34]

Medical care provided for Spanish colonial military forces was notoriously poor, soldiers often preferring jail to entering a hospital. New Spain's leading hospitals for the king's troops were the Hospital General y Militar de San Andrés (Mexico City) and the Hospital Real de San Carlos (Veracruz).[35] On the war-torn northern frontier of the viceroyalty where conflicts with the Indian created an acute need for clinical services, hospitals were not established until scandalously late in the eighteenth century.

Construction of the Hospital Militar at Chihuahua began only in

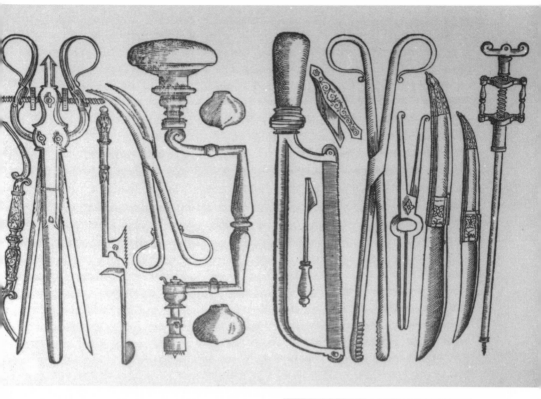

*Spanish surgical instruments from
an eighteenth-century engraving.*

1790, while a second in Coahuila was functioning by 1794. Both
operated with a skeleton staff.[36] Dr. Larrañaga sent presidial patients
to Chihuahua, but since it was outside their own province New
Mexico soldiers were individually charged for services, their bills
being entered against their future salaries by the royal treasury
officials.[37]

Something of a maverick, Dr. Larrañaga's long term in New
Mexico was punctuated with controversy and legal difficulties.
Notable events in his career included a hurried mission to the plains
in an effort to save the life of Comanche Chief Ecueracapa, a Spanish

ally, in 1793; and, the introduction of smallpox vaccine to New Mexicans, as part of the humanitarian Royal Expedition launched by the Spanish government in 1803 to take vaccination to all the colonies.[38] Larrañaga deserves a biographer.

New Mexico's representative to the Spanish cortes, Don Pedro Bautista Pino, delivered a report to that body meeting at Cádiz in 1812. He strongly criticized the government for neglecting his province, singling out for particular mention the lack of a medical facility, and the long dependence upon a single military doctor assigned to the Santa Fe presidio. Most of his fellow citizens, Pino lamented, were forced to rely on native cures.[39] That was still the case when independence arrived a decade later.

The problems colonial New Mexico faced in gaining access to regular medicine were mirrored in the other northern districts of New Spain, and probably in all of the remote provinces of the Spanish Empire.

CHAPTER FIVE

THE GREAT SMALLPOX
EPIDEMIC, 1780–1781

Today, with smallpox conquered, the memory of past epidemics that ravaged entire populations is fast fading away. During the last sixty years of the colonial regime, New Spain suffered through five general smallpox epidemics. The one that began in Mexico City in 1779, which produced an estimated 18,000 fatalities, had spread throughout the land by the following year. In the northern Borderlands, New Mexico experienced a devastating blow from the disease, as did Comanches and other adjacent Indian tribes. Owing to the scarcity of data, the impact of the epidemic upon the provincial economy and society cannot be measured now, except in general terms.

ANYONE who carefully surveys the history of colonial New Mexico must be struck by the frequent references to epidemic disease. Periodic waves of sickness swept over the province carrying off hundreds of citizens, both Indian and Spanish, and seriously disrupting the lives of survivors. If only from the social and economic standpoint, infectious disorders were extremely costly. In evaluating losses, we must go even further and take into account the psychological effects produced by the epidemics that devastated the New Mexico settlements with relentless regularity.

Apparently no decade in the eighteenth century was entirely free from a major plague of one variety or another. And yet the history of epidemiology in New Mexico remains an untapped field.[1] Surprisingly little is known of the extent and virulence of the prevailing illnesses, but if the tragic story could be told in full, it would no doubt reveal much information on such topics as settlement patterns, fluctuations of populations, and mission history. The present paper attempts no such ambitious undertaking. Rather it focuses on a single case—the great smallpox epidemic of 1780 to 1781.

Of the several afflictions plaguing New Mexico in colonial times, none was as constant or as fatal as smallpox. Variola, its technical name, is an acute infectious disease distinguished by high fever and eruptions of the skin that leave severe disfiguring scars. It strikes individuals of all ages, passing by direct contact, but the young, the old, and the undernourished are the most susceptible.

Those surviving an attack of smallpox obtained the gift of life-long immunity, which explains in part why the disease tended to occur in cycles—after a widespread epidemic, a period of years is needed for an unprotected population to grow up.[2] In the early eighteenth century, inoculation appeared in Europe and within several decades was known in the Viceroyalty of New Spain.[3] This technique involved transplanting pus from the pustules of a smallpox victim into an incision in the skin of a healthy person. The resultant infection was ordinarily mild and chances for survival far greater than in cases of infection through ordinary contact.[4] For various reasons, inoculation never became popular in Central Mexico, and it is doubtful if it was employed at all in New Mexico during colonial times.[5]

In 1799 Edward Jenner published the results of his experiments, which demonstrated that a person vaccinated with cowpox material would thereafter be immune from smallpox.[6] His evidence was so conclusive that vaccination rapidly spread around the world and within five years had been introduced even into the remote province of New Mexico.[7] As of 1780, however, the people of the Upper Rio Grande Valley had little or no protection from the ravages of this terrible disease.

Without physicians or precise knowledge of the pathology of smallpox, the afflicted in New Mexico were obliged to fall back upon their own pitifully inadequate home remedies and herbal formulas. They sought the spiritual consolation of the Church as a matter of course. In times of epidemics the clergy did more than administer the last rites and bury the dead; they did their best to alleviate the distress of their congregations by serving as friar-physicians.

That they were largely ineffectual may be attributed, not to lack of zeal, but to inadequate medical knowledge and the scarcity of pharmaceutical supplies. With the meager means at hand, the priests administered simple medicines and practiced phlebotomy, or bleeding, of patients. For a time in the seventeenth century, a kind of hospital was even maintained at San Felipe Pueblo by the Franciscan fathers, but the relief it provided during a severe epidemic must have been negligible.[8]

Although outbreaks of smallpox occurred regularly during the eighteenth century, the remaining records indicate that the epidemic of 1780–1781 proved most disastrous, causing great loss of life and producing severe dislocations in society and in the missionary program. Unhappily, only a few details of this frightful tragedy survive, although the information that can be gleaned from the records does convey some impression of the impact that smallpox had on colonial life.

The first portent of disaster appeared in late spring of 1780 with a flare-up of smallpox in the larger towns. Albuquerque was among those hardest hit, for thirty-one of its citizens succumbed to the pestilence.[9] Throughout the summer and into autumn, the number of cases steadily declined, and it perhaps seemed as if the disease had spent its fury. But a second and more virulent onrush was just around the corner.

At the beginning of January 1781, Father Juan José Hinojosa at San Felipe Pueblo wrote tersely in the margin of his burial register, "This year smallpox is expected."[10] All too soon the ominous prediction was to prove justified.

Again the larger population centers were to receive the first shocks, as the sickness crept up the Rio Grande Valley. In Santa Fe, 142 victims were claimed in January and February before the epidemic tapered off in early March. The crest was perhaps reached on February 21 when the parish priest gave up trying to list the deceased individually in his register and recorded the woeful toll in numbers only: "On this day I gave ecclesiastical burial to fifteen souls—ten adults and five children."[11] It was proper under ordinary circumstances for persons to be buried the day after death, but under pressure of the epidemic, many had to be consigned to the ground the same day as their passing.

The presidial garrison in Santa Fe suffered along with the rest of the population. Fortunately, most of the soldiers were absent during the height of the distress, but the governor reported on February 1 that twelve of those who remained in Santa Fe had fallen ill.[12] By the end of the month a total of twenty-seven had come down with the disease, and several burial certificates still exist wherein the military chaplain, Father Juan Bermejo, records that he gave ecclesiastical burial in the military chapel, Our Lady of Light, to such and such a soldier, a victim of smallpox.[13] Several other deaths were reported among the troops during the month of March, including that of a soldier who had contracted smallpox and died in Santa Cruz de la Cañada.[14]

The mournful tolling of church bells continued to be heard downriver at Albuquerque where nineteen persons, fifteen adults and

*During epidemics, bells tolled
constantly for the dead.*

four children, died between January 9 and February 6.[15] On the latter date, the burial entries abruptly ceased.

In spite of the misery in the Spanish towns, the real brunt of the sickness fell on the Indian pueblos. At Sandia, north of Albuquerque, the priest ticked off the names of the dead as they were carried to their graves, and in the margin of his parish book he recorded the cause of death in each case: *De B—(De Viruelas)*. Then he hurried on to tend the afflicted in the neighboring Spanish communities of Bernalillo, Alameda, and Corrales.[16]

At San Felipe, where Father Hinojosa had expressed fear of small-pox at the beginning of the year, 130 deaths were noted for February alone.[17] Equally appalling were the counts from the pueblos farther north. At Santo Domingo 230 Indians, young and old, died during February and the first week of March.[18] Neighboring Cochiti regis-tered 106 deaths, including those of several Spaniards from nearby farming settlements.[19] At Santa Clara the priest headed his burial register for the year 1781 with the words *Abundanzia de Biruelas* (Abundance of Smallpox) and then proceeded to fill the pages with the names of the 106 persons, Spanish and Indian, who perished.[20]

By late March or early April, the force of the epidemic began to subside along the Rio Grande, though cases continued to appear through October. Out on the periphery of the province, however, the pestilence gathered new strength with Pecos Pueblo on the east, and the Zuni and Hopi villages on the west, suffering the ravages of the disease to the end of the year.

Bancroft claims that a total of 5,025 Pueblo Indians died in the terrible sickness.[21] Neither this figure nor those cited above tell us how many people actually contracted smallpox. The fatality rate in an epidemic usually ranged from 10 to 50 percent of those infected.[22] It is known, however, that practically 100 percent of persons not immune will acquire the disease when exposed.[23] Therefore we may assume that the mortality statistics represent only a fraction of those afflicted in New Mexico during the period 1780–1781.

Late in the year 1781, Commandant General Teodoro de Croix assessed the damage caused by the pestilence and judged that because of the great reduction of population in many Indian villages, the number of missions should be reduced by consolidation.[24] The friars, always loath to yield ground, protested this directive, but to no effect since practical necessity dictated the retrenchment policy.

The extent to which the epidemic influenced other spheres of provincial life can only be guessed. The loss of many young men and women in their prime certainly caused a drain on the labor force and must have placed a severe strain on numerous households. This was true for both Indians and Spaniards. Lacking immunity, the Pueblo people were particularly susceptible to smallpox, and their mode of

Smallpox ravaged Pueblo villages like this one in 1780.

living, crowded together in closed, airless rooms, probably hastened the spread of the disease once it appeared. There are indications that the pueblos on the edges of the province suffered even more from the pestilence. This may have been the reason why Pecos, Zuni, and the Hopi pueblos were granted special tax exemptions in the years following 1782.[25]

When we examine the outbreak of 1780–1781, the question arises as to the direction from which the disease entered New Mexico. In the summer of 1779 there had been a major epidemic in Central Mexico, which ravaged the cities and countryside for a year.[26] From here smallpox might have been carried northward by travelers to the Rio Grande. Nevertheless, it is highly possible that the sickness came to New Mexico by way of the tribes of the Southern Plains. As early as 1778, an epidemic that had wrought havoc among the Indians of the Mississippi Valley, was transmitted to peoples living on the Upper Missouri.[27] In the same year the pox swept through Louisiana and into Texas, where a friar reportedly took advantage of the calamity to baptize frightened Indians and save their souls.[28] By 1780 the disease had spread to Lipan Apache of southern and western Texas, and there is good reason to believe that southern bands of the Comanche also were victims of the plague.[29] These tribes easily could have introduced smallpox into the settlements along the upper Rio Grande.[30]

Thus New Mexico's scourge of smallpox in the early 1780s may have originated either from the south or the east. It is also possible that the epidemic was a spontaneous outburst, which can occur in districts where the disease exists endemically in a mild form. Periodically, as new generations appear, the sickness assumes a sudden virulence and attacks those lacking immunity.[31] The frequency of smallpox in New Mexico suggests that it may have been endemic, although the paucity of specific records precludes a definitive judgment. Whatever its source, the pestilence of 1780–1781 was a major tragedy for colonial New Mexicans. ◈

CHAPTER SIX

ORIGINS OF PUBLIC HEALTH

According to the familiar aphorism, Cleanliness is next to Godliness. While the saying is old, the practice of personal hygiene is a relatively late development in the Western World. As recently as one hundred fifty years ago, bathing was no more than an annual event in many households. Hispanic New Mexicans, like English and French colonists, faced huge obstacles in obtaining sufficient and safe food and water for their families and in disposing of domestic waste. The idea gradually arose in the nineteenth century that actively promoting public health could benefit all sectors of society.

O NE of the many aspects of New Mexico history overlooked by scholars is the subject of personal hygiene and sanitation among the Hispanic population, from the colonial period through the nineteenth century. Virtually no mention of it, for example, can be found in Myrtle Greenfield's *A History of Public Health in New Mexico*.[1] This topic, falling within the general category of social history, has ramifications for studies in demography, medicine, economics, and even folklore. The brief introduction to the subject offered here should, therefore, cast useful light on some clouded areas of New Mexico's past.

Speaking of the western world in general, French historian Fernand Braudel observes that: "Bodily cleanliness left much to be desired at all periods and for everyone."[2] In truth, before the nineteenth century, few people paid serious attention to personal hygiene. Such basic practices as regular bathing, brushing of teeth, combing of hair, and routine changing and washing of clothing were not part of the daily life of the masses. On the unsanitary conditions in colonial America, Charles Francis Adams, Jr., has remarked, "the earliest times in New England were not pleasant . . . the earlier generations were not pleasant to live with."[3] The historical record often speaks of the filthiness of the underclasses, but usually the privileged class was just as derelict in matters of sanitation.

Maintaining cleanliness in an urban situation is dependent upon the availability of abundant pure water and an efficient distribution system, together with a feasible method of sewage disposal. In the American West, modern water and sewage systems and similar public health conveniences were a product of the second half of the nineteenth century. Santa Fe, for instance, got its first piped water system in 1881 when a private company dammed the small Santa Fe River in the canyon above town and began selling water to residents.[4] A community water works commenced operation at Albuquerque in

1883.[5] Still, until well into the twentieth century, many New Mexicans—both those on the fringes of cities and towns and those in rural settings—remained wedded to traditional methods of water procurement and human waste disposal.

From the days of earliest settlement, the Spanish residents of New Mexico, following the example of their Pueblo Indian neighbors, obtained water for domestic use from rivers, streams, irrigation ditches, springs, or ephemeral pools of rainwater and snowmelt. Occasionally, where ground water lay close to the surface, they sank shallow wells.[6] Both Hispanic and Indian women spent a significant amount of work time transporting water from these sources to the home, commonly in the early morning and evening.

Water was normally carried in large Indian-made jars (*tinajas*), or sometimes in wooden buckets, and borne on the head. A second jar might be held in the hands. The women used a gourd ladle to fill the tinajas, pouring the water through a horsehair strainer or piece of cloth to filter it. That represented the only attempt at purification. The jar had better balance on the head after filling. The dipper served as a cap on the jar during the walk home, keeping dust and insects from the water.[7]

Much of this water was contaminated with harmful aquatic organisms, such as species of intestinal bacteria and protozoa, that produced disease in humans. Most prevalent were gastrointestinal infections transmitted by such impure water. The dehydration and anemia associated with these infections were major causes of infant mortality. The soldiers of General Stephen W. Kearny, who seized Santa Fe in 1846, were particularly prone to the debilitating effects of infectious diarrhea, gastritis, and colic, which in part were transmitted by local water and food.[8]

When women reached home with their tinajas, the water jars were placed on the floor, or in some Pueblo houses on a wooden stand by the door, one made of a small tree trunk planted upright in the dirt floor, the stubs of its branches cradling the receptacle. Family members and others drank from the common jar using a dipper.[9] In a like manner, the poorer folk took their meals seated on the floor, using tortillas to dip from a common kettle of chile stew or beans. Such sharing of water and food must have facilitated the spread of communicable disease.

After diarrhea, respiratory infections were the most plentiful malady, a situation persisting since prehistoric times.[10] George Wilkins Kendall, passing the night in a crowded rural residence on the Pecos River in 1841, paints a vivid picture of the effects of pulmonary ailments.

> Every member of the family, which consisted of a grandfather and grandmother with their children and their children's children, seemed to be badly affected by a cold, or worse—for the younger branches were all evidently afflicted with the worst form of the whooping-cough. The grown people appeared to have the most distressing coughs to match their colds, while the children seemed at times to be in perfect convulsions. Occasionally the distressing sounds would all die away; anon, one of the children would begin coughing frightfully, another would join in the discordant din, and immediately the whole family were in full chorus—and thus they barked away the hours.[11]

Large families of the poor were in the habit of sleeping crowded together upon unwashed sheepskins spread on the floor of small, unventilated rooms. British traveler George Frederick Ruxton in the middle nineteenth century tells of stopping at the pueblo of Pojoaque north of Santa Fe and being put to bed on the floor amid fifteen men, women, and children, "in a space of less than that number of square feet." And, he adds wryly, "Just over my head were roosting several fowls."[12] A few days later, he halted for the night at a one-room house near Arroyo Hondo. It too contained some fifteen persons, six of whom were down with the measles.[13]

Such routine crowding, sometimes in the company of chickens, was not conducive to the maintenance of good health. The only relief came in the summer months when people customarily dragged their bedding outside and slept in the streets. This was done, said one soldier in 1846, so as "to give them free circulation of air instead of the confined atmosphere of their rooms."[14] Under the prevailing conditions, it was little wonder that young Susan Magoffin, who came to New Mexico with her trader-husband in the wake of General Kearny's invading army, should exclaim that, "sickness is great in [this] country."[15]

While foreign visitors, American and European, referred disparagingly to the widespread uncleanliness of the New Mexicans, the reality was perhaps not quite as bleak as they painted it. At every level of society existed housekeepers who took pride in their homes and did their best, under primitive conditions, to keep dirt and insects at bay and provide a livable environment for their families. Enjoying greatest success at this endeavor were members of the gentry, the *gente fina*, who numbered 1 to 2 percent of the total population. They had spacious residences, furniture (including bedsteads with mattresses), and an abundance of servants available for cooking, water carrying, and cleaning.

The poorest housewife, however, had the means to maintain even the most modest of dwellings. White clay or gypsum was available for whitewashing interior walls. Bedding and clothing could be regularly aired, or washed in the neighboring irrigation ditch. And packed-dirt floors were periodically swept and sprinkled with water to keep down dust.

In the latter regard, it can be noted that the Spanish broom (*escoba*) was the most ubiquitous household cleaning device. It was simply and quickly manufactured of sacaton, a perennial bunchgrass found throughout the area.[16] Stalks were bound tightly in a round sheaf and without a handle, more like a whiskbroom, so that the sweeper was required to bend from the waist. Charles F. Lummis, who saw it used in the last century, declared: "It is never used dry; the housewife always dips the end in a dish of water to lay the dust."[17] One of Kearny's troopers thought these small brooms "rather neat and pretty."[18]

Interior rooms, entryways, courtyards (*placitas*), and the street in front of the residence received a daily sweeping, if the housekeeper were diligent. She probably also owned several *escobetillas*, even smaller versions of the broom, which served to brush the hair and were perhaps employed, as in Indian custom, to clean the stone metates after grinding corn. When not in use, the broom stood at the edge of the hearth, next to the corner fireplace.

In addition to water and grass brooms, the detergent qualities of soap were required. Little attention has been given to soap manufacture in New Mexico, or the allied industry of candle making, both of which utilized tallow as their principal ingredient. Hispanic settlers were well supplied with buffalo and sheep tallow, rendered in large copper kettles over open fires.[19] Huge quantities of this animal by-product went into candles, many being exported to northern Mexico for illuminating mines and churches. In New Mexico, tallow was mixed with resin to form the chief lubricant for cart wheels and mining and ore-processing equipment, and was also combined with pine pitch to produce homemade tar. The remainder was consigned to the soap kettles.

Besides the fatty acids of tallow, soapmaking required the addition of caustic potash, obtained on the Hispanic frontier by leaching the ashes of green cottonwood, ash, or corncobs.[20] The resulting lye solution, when boiled with tallow, reacted to produce a soft brown soap (*jabón de lejía*). Addition of soda at critical stages in the production process gave a hard (or Castile) soap that could be poured, while still hot, into large square wooden molds and afterward cut into individual bars. Few descriptions of this task exist for New Mexico. Mainly, it seems to have been in the hands of older women, who were also the candlemakers.[21]

Documentary references to soap are widely scattered through the colonial years. One of the first, in 1631, indicates that each Franciscan friar received an allotment of three pesos' worth upon arrival of the triennial mission supply caravan from Mexico City.[22] That is an inconsequential amount, and some evidence exists that the friars developed their own "soap works" within the complex of mission shops.[23]

The citizenry in that early period were thrown on their own resources, but nothing has come to light so far that would establish precisely when soapmaking emerged as a cottage industry. Prosperous New Mexican merchants and business agents for the governors who traveled to Parral in southern Chihuahua (then Nueva Vizcaya) could have purchased bars of hard soap to bring home. An inventory of a Parral shopkeeper in 1641 shows on hand, "222 small bars of soap, worth a total of 7 pesos."[24] The modest original price of that soap, however, would have been increased several times by high transportation costs had it been imported from Chihuahua to New Mexico.

In the late colonial period, soldiers of the royal presidio at Santa Fe received a twice monthly ration of soap, which presumably was locally made.[25] Other mentions of soap are rare, and good quality hard soap probably remained a scarce commodity. Later in the nineteenth century, bar soap was shipped over the Santa Fe Trail from Missouri.[26] An apparent low level of native soap production in New Mexico may have been owing to the availability of natural substitutes.

One of these, obtained in the vicinity of Zia Pueblo northeast of Albuquerque, was *tierra jabón*. The identity of this mineral is questionable, but it may have been powdered soapstone. It was described in 1779 as having the color of soap and working very well to wash clothes.[27] No subsequent mentions of tierra jabón have been found, so its use likely did not extend beyond the colonial period.

Amole, or yucca root, was another soap substitute widely favored by Hispanics and Indians. Indeed, its use continues in isolated areas to the present day. Among the several varieties of the plant, *Yucca glauca*, or small soapweed yucca, which grows throughout the Southwest, was the one commonly collected by women.[28] The roots were pounded, either fresh or dried, to separate the strong, spongy mass of fibers. Thrashing the pulverized root in water released the substance saponin and produced a rich, soapy lather.

As a detergent for washing woolens, amole won wide acclaim. Both men and women preferred it as a shampoo, since it gave their hair a lustrous sheen. And, its cleansing properties worked well in both cold water and hard water. Like yucca, the prolific wild gourd plant (*Cucurbita digitata*) contained saponin, and the New Mexicans often utilized the roots and gourds as soap and as a bleaching agent.[29]

That cleaning materials were available to the New Mexicans, of course, was no indicator of their frequency or intensity of use. The strictness of personal hygiene and sanitation must have varied considerably from one individual and household to another. Some poorer families, for instance, seldom changed clothes (a single set being perhaps all they owned), and the children were literally sewn into their garments, wearing them until they fell to pieces.

Still, laundry day, with women and girls gathering on the banks of streams or irrigation ditches, was an event noted in the journals of newcomers. The laundresses transported large bundles of clothing, bedding, and rugs on their heads to the site, where water was boiled in kettles and then poured into a long log trough (*tablón*), to which was added amole or soap. Rinsing was done in the stream or ditch, and perhaps a final pounding was performed between smooth stones to remove stubborn stains. The laundry was spread on the grass to dry, "as young Roman girls do along the Tiber," noted Susan Wallace in the 1880s.[30] Then it was folded and carried home in bundles or in Indian baskets of willow osiers.[31] One American remarked that pads of yucca fiber that had yielded amole could always be found scattered about the water places after washday.[32]

In traditional New Mexican society, washing and bathing as habits of cleanliness seem to have been sparingly practiced. As in other parts of the world, the masses may have held the suspicion that baths, particularly in winter, posed a health hazard. Homes were not equipped for bathing, nor have references surfaced to specialized tubs for that purpose. The clergy and perhaps some members of the upper class owned metal wash basins, but even there, one looks in vain for any mention of towels.[33] In warm weather, occasional outdoor bathing at the water sources occurred, but more for refreshment then cleansing. The practice doubtless added to the pollution of drinking water.

New Mexico's numerous hot springs, whose waters were thought to possess medicinal properties, long attracted bathers, but for therapeutic rather than hygienic reasons. Rheumatism, arthritis, and skin ailments, especially, appeared to respond favorably to soaking in the springs.[34] The Pueblo Indians for centuries had appreciated the healing value of these thermal springs. Moreover, they frequently resorted to sweat baths, for therapeutic as well as ceremonial purposes.[35]

Lack of cleanliness evidently contributed to a general infestation of such disease vectors as lice, bedbugs, fleas, mites, and flies. The pueblos were plagued by vermin long before Europeans arrived. Evidence of head lice, for instance, has been found archaeologically on the scalps of desiccated Indian remains at prehistoric burial sites.[36] New Mexico's first colonists, occupying a Tewa pueblo, renamed San Gabriel, were literally driven from their quarters by pests.

A report of 1601 indicates:

> The people leave their houses to sleep in their small vegetable gardens in order to escape the unbearable plague of bedbugs. Furthermore, there are an infinite number of field mice, which breed a species of lice, the pain from whose sting lasts for almost twenty-four hours.[37]

Bishop Pedro Tamarón of Durango, inspecting the New Mexico missions more than a century and a half later, encountered swarms of bedbugs at another Tewa pueblo, Nambé.[38] Such chance references in the colonial period merely hint at the magnitude of a problem that was more fully described by American observers in the nineteenth century.

Kendall, at the village of San Miguel in 1841, complained that his room was completely "overrun with *chinches* [bedbugs], which when night came, issued from every crack and crevice in the walls."[39] Later, in El Paso he remarked that the lower orders of Mexico were generally infested with lice and other vermin.[40]

When General Kearny entered and occupied Santa Fe, his soldiers were dismayed to discover that the entire town was lousy. "There is a universal presence of vermin on the bodies of all the inhabitants," lamented volunteer Frank S. Edwards.[41] All of the public and private buildings, including the few hotels, were heavily infested. Another soldier a few years later quipped that in some of the houses of the gentry, "a traveler can lose a pint of blood in a night."[42]

It must not be supposed, however, that New Mexicans surrendered to insect pests without a fight. In Spain poor folk whitewashed the interior walls of buildings in the belief that the practice kept vermin at bay.[43] Whitewashing was also the custom on the upper Rio Grande but apparently to little effect. The inevitable cracks and crevices found in adobe walls and the narrow splits that opened in roof beams as they dried provided a safe refuge for all manner of insect life. In desperation, women boiled the wild gourd in water, which was then placed in pans throughout the home. They hoped the horrible, fetid odor of the water would drive out the pests.[44]

Bedbugs teemed in blankets and sheepskins, while body lice, when not feeding, attached themselves and their eggs to the fibers of clothing. Bedding and garments, therefore, had to be removed periodically for cleansing. Proper laundering effectively evicted the invaders, but another method proved equally useful. Indians, Hispanics, and American trappers routinely spread clothing and blankets on an anthill. The ants were very fond of lice and quickly consumed the entire population.[45]

Removal of body and head lice involved a never-ending struggle. Confederate private Henry Clay Wright, imprisoned at Santa Fe after the battle of Glorieta in 1862, soon became lousy. His remedy was to scrub down with lye soap.[46] Some New Mexicans also may have used that method, but generally the natives simply picked off the pests, one by one, from their persons.

Vendors in the open market on the Santa Fe plaza spent idle moments plucking lice and nits from the hair. The catch was crushed between the thumbnails, producing an audible pop. Frank S. Edwards spoke of the practice with disgust: "It is not unusual to see women and men stop suddenly, expertly hunt [vermin], and a sharp sound announces to you a death—while the next minute they handle the fruit or cheese which they are offering to sell you."[47] Richard S. Elliott, one of Edwards's contemporaries, complained upon a stopover in the village of Galisteo, that "the people quite coolly pick off vermin in the presence of visitors."[48]

These remarks notwithstanding, many rural folk were embarrassed

Delousing.

to be seen delousing in public. Groups of women would gather in a home or sunny yard to delouse one another and their children. But should a man approach, the activity ceased until he went on his way again.[49] Such gatherings, attended by merry conversation, were regarded as social occasions.

In 1856 the territorial attorney William W. H. Davis called attention to another insect problem. At Albuquerque, he said, "there are flies and mosquitoes, which swarm in and out of doors in untold millions, which neither day nor night allow man or beast to live in peace."[50] Both pests were disease carriers, but the populace was unaware of that and exerted only small efforts to control them. In the absence of flyswatters, a small leafy cottonwood branch might be used to shoo flies from the table. One Hispano woman is reported to have beaten a metal pan on the theory that the noise would drive flying insects from her home. Some people burned cow dung in the yard, believing that the smoke warded off mosquitoes. Americans, arriving on the Santa Fe Trail, seem to have introduced the first mosquito nets for sleeping. But their use was not adopted by the native population.[51]

One of the chief factors affecting personal hygiene is the problem of human waste disposal. Careless handling of waste can propagate a variety of diseases. For centuries, Europeans were in the habit of throwing the contents of their chamber pots and kitchen slops out the window, so that their streets were open sewers.[52] Larger cities had public latrines, some of them extending over rivers or streams which carried away the excreta. Others were built upon cesspits, with the ordure periodically removed and taken to fertilize surrounding fields.[53] In the cities and towns of Spain, "toilet facilities were of the most primitive kind, and the streets were invariably dotted with defecation and urine," according to one writer. "The Spaniards who came to the New World were amazed by the cleanliness of the Indian towns as compared with their own."[54]

While in New Mexico, Pedro de Castañeda, chronicler of the Coronado expedition, observed that: "The [Pueblo] villages are free of nuisances because they go outside to excrete, and they pass their water into clay vessels, which they empty at a distance from the village."[55] Three and a half centuries later, in 1880, archaeologist-historian Adolph F. Bandelier found the practice still intact. At Santo Domingo Pueblo, for instance, he noted: "On every roof there was the tinaja [jar] with the urine of the night, which smelt ugly. They carry it out into the fields."[56] The building of outhouses with cesspits in the pueblos did not become common until well after World War I. Zia Pueblo was reported to be without latrines as late as 1924.[57]

To what degree the Hispanic settlers emulated the Pueblo Indians in their careful disposal of waste is uncertain, simply because mention of that delicate matter occurs infrequently in the documents. The Franciscan missionaries usually had latrines within their conventos, or living quarters, attached to the church, but those in-house sanitary arrangements are practically the only ones referred to in the colonial documents. At the mission of Tajique Pueblo in 1663, toilets existed in the convento and were used by Indians as well as the friars.[58] At Picurís Pueblo, 1747, the convento had "an upper room for privies, roofed, with its two-seat box." But at Acoma, the latrine was located in a corner of the convento's open courtyard and was described in

1776 by Father Atanasio Domínguez as "a small recess for certain necessary business."[59]

How these facilities were maintained and their contents regularly emptied is left unrecorded. Possibly, as was done elsewhere, the friars dumped wood ashes in the privy holes to serve as a chemical reagent.[60] They also may have furnished the latrines with corncobs, for use in place of toilet paper, as was the custom in some parts of New Spain.

Ignoring the example of the missionaries, the Indians until recent times continued to remove human waste in their tinajas on a daily basis, in effect a more hygienic system. A similar practice seems to have been followed by much of the Hispanic population. At least there is little evidence at present to indicate the existence of freestanding privies or in-house chambers functioning as latrines, in the traditional domestic setting.

Rural New Mexicans probably were accustomed to relieving themselves in the great outdoors, but like their urban neighbors they must have also owned a chamber pot (*bacín*) for use inside during cold weather. The accepted procedure was to dispose of waste from chamber pots on farmland. That was feasible even in a town the size of Santa Fe, which had a population of approximately 5,000 at the end of the colonial period, because fields intruded to the very center of the community. Notwithstanding, there must have been abundant occasions when waste was tossed into the streets or the open irrigation ditches, since the nature of infection and dangers of contamination were not then known.

Curiously, however, the early Anglo-Americans seldom complained about sewage and odors in the streets of New Mexican towns. One explanation could be that their own home places suffered from the same pollution, so that the situation did not appear unusual enough to invite comment. But another possibility is that the streets were kept relatively clean of human and animal waste by stray chickens, pigs, and especially dogs, which are all consumers of dung. The cleansing process may have also been aided by the strong New Mexico sun and wind which tend to dry up bodily wastes quickly.[61]

The widespread use of chamber pots in New Mexican homes has to be inferred from a few casual references and from what is known generally about Hispanic customs of waste disposal. Wills and inventories from the northern frontier of New Spain, sometimes mention pots of copper or even silver.[62] But unquestionably the largest number were ceramic. Their characteristics included a cylindrical form, either straight or tapered, a lead or tin glaze with a washed-out blue design, open mouth, a wide-flared horizontal rim, and two handles.[63] Large quantities of chamber pots manufactured in Sevilla were exported to the colonies in the sixteenth century, but within a short time ceramics industries in Mexico City and Puebla were supplying New Spain with its needs. While some of the finely made Mexican chamber pots are known to have reached the northern borderlands, the average citizen on the frontier depended upon cheap vessels, locally produced. The New Mexicans, fragmentary evidence would suggest, relied chiefly upon Pueblo potters for their chamber pots.[64]

The responsibility for sanitation and public health was shared by officials at all levels within the Spanish empire.[65] Included among royal ordinances, codified by Philip II in 1573, was a general provision that towns of New Spain be founded in "an elevated place where there are healthy conditions."[66] Once established, municipal governments took charge of public health matters and passed local ordinances to protect the water supply, keep the streets clean, and govern the maintenance of cemeteries.[67] No record of such ordinances during the colonial era has come to light for any of New Mexico's four villas, or munici-palities—Santa Fe, Albuquerque, Santa Cruz de la Cañada, and El Paso. But during the Mexican period, enlightened public health meas-ures were adopted at Santa Fe by the *ayuntamiento*, or city council.

In 1829, for example, the council assigned one of its members to serve as an overseer (*mayordomo*) for maintaining the cleanliness and order of the streets. When in 1833 the municipal body learned that cholera was raging in the East and that it might reach Santa Fe, intro-duced by trail traffic, it proposed establishment of a sanitary board to deal with the emergency. And it urged the governor to halt for a

*Spanish majolica slop jar or
chamber pot from the eighteenth
century.*
Museum of New Mexico photograph
neg. no. 66200

*Rubbish piled in front of a Santa
Fe house.*
Museum of New Mexico photograph
neg. no. 20844

forty-day period all wagon caravans from the United States, until their cargoes could be fumigated outside the settlements.[68]

The same year the council issued a comprehensive proclamation on city government, written by its legal adviser, Don Antonio Barreiro, which incorporated progressive measures on public health and safety. New regulations required draining of stagnant pools, cleaning of streets, and removal of garbage. Burning of rubbish piles was prohibited, to prevent air pollution, and the throwing of trash and dead animals into irrigation ditches and streams strictly forbidden. Two inspectors were to be appointed, their duty to examine flour and grain in the markets to ensure cleanliness. Meat sold to the public had to be suitable for human consumption and none could be vended from animals that had died of rabies. And there were additional rules in a like vein. Unfortunately, little evidence exists to suggest these measures were strictly enforced.[69]

In 1863 the Albuquerque board of aldermen passed a set of town ordinances covering animal and traffic control, sanitation, public works, zoning, and misdemeanors. Although this was done under the American territorial government, the majority of the alderman were native New Mexicans and their regulations reflected the Hispanic legal tradition. Ordinance 12, for instance, provided that "any person making water, or depositing any excrement, under any porch, or upon any sidewalk or wall in front of the plaza . . . upon conviction . . . shall be fined . . . or sentenced to imprisonment."[70]

Unlike those imposed earlier in Santa Fe, the Albuquerque measures seem to have been enforced with vigor. Soon after their enactment, the local press reported:

> Last week, Alderman Salvador Armijo did a "land office business" in the way of fining sundry individuals for offenses against town laws. The consequence will be that, when hot weather comes, a person will be able to walk through any of our streets without his nostrils being saluted by odors incompatible with the relish of a good dinner.[71]

Prior to the opening of the twentieth century, efforts by government officials go promote public health and by citizens to maintain a regimen of personal hygiene were of the most rudimentary nature. However, the conditions, practices, and policies associated with these subjects furnish useful sidelights on the functioning of traditional society in New Mexico. ◈

CHAPTER SEVEN

ATTEMPTS TO OPEN A
NEW MEXICO-SONORA ROAD

Trade in raw materials, foodstuffs, livestock, hard goods, and even Indian slaves formed the backbone of New Mexico's colonial economy. In the absence of any river or sea ports, the province was wholly dependent in its interior and exterior commerce upon the main Camino Real (Royal Road) that descended the Rio Grande Valley from Santa Fe southward to Chihuahua City, and upon its secondary branches that led eastward from the capital to the Pecos Valley, northward to Taos, and northwestward to Ojo Caliente and Abiquiu. One goal of the Spanish Bourbons in the latter 1700s was to develop new commercial roadways as a means of promoting economic growth.

I N the fall of 1644 Don Pedro de Perea, governor of the province of Sonora, arrived in Santa Fe, the capital of New Mexico. Don Pedro was seeking Spanish colonists to settle and serve as soldiers in his recently created jurisdiction. During the preceding decade, prospectors from the mining towns of Parral and Santa Barbara in Nueva Vizcaya had traveled west, crossed the Sierra Madre, and found evidence of rich silver and gold deposits near the headwaters of the Bavispe, Sonora and San Miguel rivers in northeastern Sonora. News of these discoveries was welcomed in New Mexico, for the inhabitants depended upon limited trade relations with the merchants of Parral and saw the mineral districts as possibly offering new markets for their products. Perea enlisted a dozen men to serve in Sonora and departed. During the years that followed, New Mexicans—merchants and government officials in Santa Fe—sought to develop trade contacts with Sonora, but found their efforts hampered by the absence of a highway, hostile Indians and vast distance. Although no direct road was opened between New Mexico and Sonora during Spanish times, the repeated attempts that were made to establish such a route revealed a great deal about the rugged terrain and the ongoing Apache problem on the Sonora-New Mexico border.[1]

At its establishment in 1598 by colonizer Juan de Oñate, New Mexico was the northernmost bastion of Spanish civilization on the outer rim of the Viceroyalty of New Spain. The only road out of the colony, the Camino Real, ran south from Santa Fe to El Paso del Norte on the Rio Grande, and thence down through the province of Nueva Vizcaya to Mexico City. The flourishing Franciscan missions planted among the Pueblo Indians were supplied with foodstuffs, hardware and religious equipment by triennial caravans from the vice-regal capital. From New Mexico the friar-administrators shipped out quantities of hides, jerked meat, salt, piñon nuts and cotton blankets to be sold in the mining communities of northern New Spain.[2]

Although their commercial relations were directed primarily toward settlements in neighboring Nueva Vizcaya, New Mexicans developed contacts with Sonora soon after mines and missions appeared in that province. Jesuit work began in southern Sonora in 1614 and extended as far north as Ures by 1636. Captain Pedro de Perea became chief magistrate and military commandant of Sonora in the same year, and in 1641 established the first provincial capital at the mining town of San Juan Bautista on the Moctezuma River. In his governing capacity, Perea was required to maintain twenty-five soldiers for defense of the province. Because population was small in his district, he traveled north to Santa Fe three years later in an effort to enlist the requisite number of men. There he was able to engage only twelve, eight of whom were members of the prominent family of Francisco Pérez Granillo. Although New Mexico played "a mother-agent role" in the beginnings of Sonora, the contacts between the two provinces for several decades were sporadic and temporary.[3]

News of a major silver strike in 1657 at San Juan Bautista probably prompted the next surge of interest in Sonora by New Mexicans. Three years later, at Santa Fe, Governor Bernardo Lopez de Mendizábal personally engaged Francisco Pérez Granillo to organize a pack train to carry local products to the mining districts. Pérez Granillo took seventy Apache slaves to be sold in the mines and a stock of goods—deerskins, buffalo hides, piñon nuts, salt, cloth, stockings and embroidery work—valued at 7,000 pesos.[4]

Granillo's route in 1660 is not known, but he quite possibly followed the Camino Real south to a point below El Paso, then turned west, passing the future site of Janos, and crossing the Sierra Madre into the upper Sonora valley. He disposed of the governor's merchandise according to his instructions, but apparently lingered in the settlements, perhaps visiting kinsmen or conducting business of his own. His delay there gave time for the *Audiencia* of Guadalajara to learn of the sale of the Apache slaves, a matter in direct violation of Spanish law. This legal body immediately issued a decree nullifying the transaction and ordering the trader to make a refund to the purchasers. On returning to Santa Fe, Pérez Granillo found that his sponsor, López de Mendizábal, had been removed from office. The new governor, Diego de Peñalosa, promptly confiscated the silver bullion that Pérez Granillo had received for the hides and other goods.

The activities of Bernardo Gruber, a German peddler, shed further light on early New Mexico-Sonora trade. Gruber, according to Fray Juan Bernal, a New Mexican friar, was a "strange man" who resided in the mining districts of Sonora and periodically came to New Mexico "to sell merchandise and other trifles which this kingdom lacks." Gruber doubtless learned of the commercial possibilities from former residents of New Mexico then living in Sonora and from others involved in trade with the Rio Grande pueblos. By 1666, if not earlier, he appeared in New Mexico with a train of pack mules and traveled from one village to another disposing of his wares.[5]

On April 19, 1668, Gruber was arrested by Father Juan de Paz, head of the Franciscan Order in New Mexico, and charged with sorcery. Specifically, he was accused of leading Pueblo Indians astray by giving them magical formulas intended to make them invulnerable in battle. Gruber was confined in the mission convent of Abó, and his property was seized. This consisted of seventeen pack mules, thirteen horses and mares, three Apache men and women, and an assortment of articles he had received in trade. Later, he broke out of the cell and fled toward Sonora but was killed by Apaches en route. Because of the unusual nature of this case, the details of Gruber's ill-fated trade venture have been preserved. Probably other small operators were involved in similar traffic.[6]

Another area of contact for traders from New Mexico and Sonora was the San Pedro Valley of present-day Arizona. New Mexicans began making occasional trips into the San Pedro Valley to trade with the Sobaipuris, a Piman group, by the early 1680s. Although this commerce may have been initiated some years before, it doubtless received added impetus after 1680, the year the Pueblo Indians rebelled and drove Spanish settlers from the upper Rio Grande. The survivors of that catastrophe congregated at El Paso, but after some months, it became clear there would be no immediate reconquest of

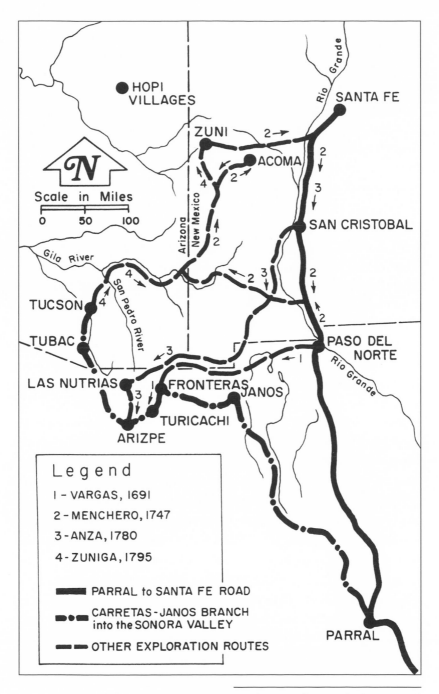

Explorers and routes in Sonora and New Mexico.

the province, and many of them moved into Nueva Vizcaya, Sonora, and Sinaloa to establish new homes. Some enlisted in the garrisons of frontier presidios, others found positions in mines or on haciendas, and a few must have engaged in trade, perhaps finding their way into Sobaipuri country.[7]

Eleven years after the revolt, General Diego de Vargas blazed a military trail from El Paso into northern Sonora. In the late fall of 1691, while gathering soldiers and colonists at El Paso to launch a campaign to reconquer the Pueblo area, Vargas learned of an outbreak of hostilities among Indians to the west, and as ranking officer on this section of the frontier, it fell to him to quiet the disturbance. In a sweeping campaign against hostile Pimas, Jocomes and Mansos and Gila Apaches, he led a combined force of New Mexican, Nueva Vizcayan, Sonoran, and Sinaloan regulars and militiamen a distance of 480 leagues from El Paso into northeastern Sonora as far as Turicachi, south of Fronteras. Vargas stated that he had explored much *terra incognita,* discovered new trails and water holes, and made first contact with groups of Sobaipuris. Some of his claims of discovery must be dismissed, however, for Indian informants told Father Eusebio Kino in the late summer of 1692 that merchant parties from both New Mexico and Sonora had passed through their country in earlier years.[8]

With the successful reconquest of the Pueblo province, the refounding of Santa Fe, and the building of new Spanish communities along the upper Rio Grande, New Mexican trade with Sonora resumed, although the most prosperous commerce continued to be with Nueva Vizcaya. In April of 1707, Governor Pedro Rodríguez Cubero and the Santa Fe cabildo issued licenses to a number of local residents to trade buffalo robes, buckskins, piñon nuts, and other commodities in Sonora and Nueva Vizcaya for horses, mules and sheep.[9]

During the first half of the eighteenth century, Sonoran missionaries manifested an interest in opening a trail north to the Hopi villages, which then lay within the political jurisdiction of New Mexico. The Spaniards had not subdued the Hopis after the revolt of 1680, and the priests hoped that better communication might facilitate their return to the church's fold. Father Kino called attention to the fact that travelers could go straight north from the San Xavier del Bac Mission, near modern Tucson, and reach the Hopi province within sixty or seventy leagues, although they would undoubtedly encounter hostile Apaches infesting the route. A royal order authorized a missionary expedition to link Pimería Alta directly to New Mexico in 1725, but nothing was done until 1743, when Father Ignacio Keller attempted to penetrate the country north of the Gila. However, he and his soldier escort turned back after a brush with Apaches. News of the incident reached the Hopis and through them was eventually carried to authorities in Santa Fe.[10]

As midcentury approached, the Spaniards became increasingly engrossed with the Apache problem, realizing fully that it must be resolved before roads and communication could be developed and the missionary program expanded. To reduce this threat, the viceroy of New Spain in 1747 ordered a campaign waged against the Gila Apaches and their allies, using soldiers from presidios in Nueva Vizcaya, Sonora, and New Mexico. A secondary objective was to explore the approaches to the provinces of the Zunis and Hopis. This effort, involving nearly 1,000 troops and Indian auxiliaries, was the first serious Spanish assault on the Western Apaches and the opening salvo in a bitter war that lasted intermittently until the end of colonial times. Because the well-known Friar Juan Miguel Menchero served as chaplain and military adviser in this undertaking, historians have referred to it as the Menchero campaign. However, Captain Alonso Victores Rubí de Celís, the presidial commander at El Paso, was commander in chief.[11]

In spite of propitious beginnings, the Spanish offensive of 1747 bore little fruit. A sudden Ute uprising in the north diverted many of the New Mexican troops, while the forces that united on the Río Mimbres to scout the headwaters of the Gila, Mimbres, and San Francisco rivers were unable to engage a significant body of the enemy. The united expedition then moved north to explore possible Apache trails into northern New Mexico, and encamped on the plains near Zuni Salt Lake. From here, Father Menchero, with a small escort, visited the pueblo of Acoma, made inquiries, and rejoined the main party, which continued to Zuni Pueblo. In December of 1747, after three months in the field, the forces were disbanded on the Rio Grande. Although it failed to accomplish its military objective, the Celís-Menchero expedition demonstrated the feasibility of a Sonora-New Mexico road along the route it had traveled. Nothing could be done, however, since the country remained securely in the grasp of the elusive Apaches.

A less ambitious venture against the Gila Apaches was launched in 1756. In that year Captain Bernardo Antonio de Bustamante y Tagle of Nueva Vizcaya and Captain Gabriel Antonio de Vildósola of Sonora rendezvoused along the headwaters of the Gila, and led a combined force of presidial soldiers and Tarahumara and Opatá auxiliaries west into the towering Sierra de Mogollón. Here, they killed some enemy warriors, and captured women and children, who as prisoners of war could be sold into slavery. The troops then returned to their respective stations. In the years that followed, the Spaniards made periodic strikes into the Gila wilderness, but their principal accomplishment was to expand knowledge of the rugged terrain along the New Mexico-Sonora border.[12]

Military forays into the heart of Apachería kept alive the interest in opening a road between the New Mexican settlements and the Sonoran missions and mines. In 1751, for example, the Marqués de Altamira, legal adviser for the Audiencia of Mexico, recommended that Spanish colonies be established in the Gila valley and to the west on the lower Colorado to serve as bases for opening roads to New Mexico and California, respectively. The prominent Franciscan, Father Francisco Garcés, during the 1770s made several reconnaissance trips northward from San Xavier del Bac toward the Hopi villages in hopes of finding a suitable highway from the Sonoran frontier into New Mexico. But when he reached the Hopis in the summer of 1776, he met with a cool reception from the still unreconciled Indians and went no farther. Before turning back, he dispatched a letter to the friar of Zuni, expressing the wish that the New Mexicans could develop a safe trade route to Sonora and send cattle thither.[13]

The governor of Sonora, Francisco Antonio Crespo, was interested in a similar plan. In 1774 he submitted a formal proposal to the viceroy, urging the subjugation of the Hopis and the marking of a road between his province and New Mexico. This suggestion reached Mexico City at a time when the Crown was demonstrating a growing interest in opening new trade and communication routes to weld together the far-flung border domain. Thus a viceregal letter, enclosing a copy of Crespo's plan, was sent to Governor Pedro Fermín de Mendinueta of New Mexico, requesting his observations. The governor gave it his immediate attention.[14]

In the fall of 1775, Mendinueta responded, outlining both the prospects and the problems involved in the laying out of a road from Santa Fe to the Gila. The governor suggested two routes: first, a route south from Zuni Pueblo (which he favored); and, second, one circling west and south by way of the Hopi towns. Going directly southward from Zuni, he wrote, travelers could reach the upper Río San Francisco within four days. Descending this river, they would pass through a fertile valley with several Apache rancherías and cultivated fields of maize. Six leagues beyond, the San Francisco united with the Gila, giving access to the Sonora frontier.

An alternate route, via the Hopis, would involve travel forty-six leagues northwest of Zuni. These Indians lived in seven well-built towns, six of them small and the seventh having a population of 800 families. In spite of being apostates, the Hopis were generally peaceful. They traded with the Zunis and on occasion with the Spaniards from whom they obtained ironware. "The distances are not great," Mendinueta stated, "nor would there be much difficulty in promoting communication between New Mexico and Sonora, provided the Apache did not interfere. But if these are at war, seldom if ever could citizens from one or the other provinces get through because whatever commerce might be established would be so small that a sufficient number of people could not be gotten together to risk it."

Governor Mendinueta's observations were not immediately implemented, and in 1777 he was succeeded by Juan Bautista de Anza, a veteran of the Sonoran frontier. Anza had gained viceregal favor by pioneering a land route from Sonora to the new settlements in California. Upon assuming office, he gave full support to the long delayed project of linking the Sonora-New Mexico provinces. In part, his interest was a personal one, since his life thus far had been dedicated to the king's service on the frontier. But practical consideration of defense and economics also guided his policy.[15]

During the second half of the eighteenth century, the Spanish colonial government launched a number of expeditions on the northern frontier in an effort to open new roads for commerce and communication. This activity followed upon the heels of Spain's acquisition of Louisiana from France in 1762 and its occupation of upper California in 1769. The border provinces stretching from the Mississippi to the Pacific were tied to the main population centers of northern Mexico by branches of the Camino Real. But east-west roads linking these provinces were non-existent. To remedy this deficiency colonial authorities sponsored a number of exploratory expeditions by military officers, friars, and private individuals. Envisioned was a network of roads that would connect New Mexico with Texas and Louisiana on the east, and another set tying New Mexico with Sonora and California on the west.[16]

As Anza probably knew, the occasional trading caravans between New Mexico and Sonora had traveled dim mountain and desert trails. The exact routes were not recorded, probably because none possessed sufficient merit to be developed as an established thoroughfare. With the rise in Apache hostility in the 1750s, punitive expeditions increasingly had penetrated the Gila wilderness and learned much about the terrain there. Like other frontier officials Anza was convinced that an accessible road through this area was a military necessity. He also felt it could prove an economic boon to both provinces.[17]

A Santa Fe-Sonora road, he was quoted as saying in 1780, would insure "an end to the grievous and dishonest trade which has been carried on with the province of Nueva Vizcaya." By this he was referring to the long-standing monopoly enjoyed by the Chihuahuan merchants over New Mexico's commerce, made possible by the fact that they were situated on the only thoroughfare out of the province.

Juan Bautista de Anza, soldier, explorer, and Spanish governor of New Mexico.
Museum of New Mexico
photograph neg. no. 50828

Anza also felt that a road to Sonora would provide access to the coast, where New Mexicans could procure European goods at less cost. Such a road might also encourage New Mexicans to go and work in the Sonora silver mines, where a labor shortage existed owing to recent emigration to California. Finally, Anza believed the proposed highway would be of great strategic importance in future Apache campaigns and also would ease his problems of communication with his military superior, the commandant general of the Interior Provinces, whose headquarters were in the Sonoran town of Arizpe.

When Governor Anza assumed office, the New Mexico-Sonora trade, such as it was, followed a long, roundabout route. From Santa Fe, merchants traveled the Camino Real south to El Paso, where they branched off on a secondary trail running southwest across the plains of Nueva Vizcaya. South of the Hatchet Mountains, and just below the present New Mexico line, the route forked. One arm turned south to the presidios of Janos and San Buenaventura in northern Nueva

Vizcaya. The other angled northwestward into the New Mexico panhandle, passed through San Luís Pass (separating the San Luís and Animas mountains), crossed the Llanos de San Luis (Animas Valley), at that time the beginning of the jurisdiction of Sonora, and led down Guadalupe Canyon to San Bernadino, where a presidio existed between 1775 and 1780. At this point travelers could go south to Fronteras and Arizpe, or continue westward to the San Pedro River and the road leading to the northernmost outposts in Pimería Alta.[18]

In casting about for a more direct road to Sonora, Anza considered several possibilities. One route might follow the well-marked trail westward from the Rio Grande settlements via Zuni to the land of the Hopis. From there a way possibly could be found south through the mountains of central Arizona to the Spanish outposts at Tucson and Tubac below the Gila River. Unfortunately, the route via the Hopis was as long as the road running west from El Paso. In fact, a royal cosmographer in 1776 had estimated that the direct distance from Santa Fe to the Presidio of Tubac was 243 common leagues, but that with inevitable detours and a swing through the Hopi country, the traveling leagues would be about 300. A second possible route would run from the Zuni pueblos south through the valley of the Río San Francisco to its junction with the Gila. This path had been blazed by Father Menchero in 1747 and recommended by Governor Mendinueta in 1775.[19]

By the fall of 1780 Anza settled on a third and wholly different route. Earlier in the year he had conducted a relief expedition to the Hopis, who were suffering from a prolonged drought, and apparently assessed the merits of a road through that country and discarded the idea. Disadvantages of the Río San Francisco route were the rugged terrain, which precluded the use of wagons and carts, and the concentration of Apache rancherías along the river. Anza's third choice seemed the most logical. From Santa Fe, it ran down the Rio Grande south of Socorro, swung west and south around the Black Range and the Mimbres Mountains, skirted several lesser sierras, crossed a desert plain, then bore directly through the Chiricahua Mountains toward the presidio of Santa Cruz de las Nutrias, near the headwaters of the

Spanish pack train on a mountain trail.
From: J. Russell Bartlett, *Personal Narrative* [1854]

San Pedro River in northeastern Sonora. If a road could be carved through this region, Anza felt the distance from his province to Sonora could be reduced to less than 150 leagues.[20]

Several military expeditions had previously entered this part of southern New Mexico hunting Apaches, and colonial citizens probably had crossed it from time to time on their way to the markets and mines of Sonora. When Bishop Pedro Tamarón was at Bacerac, in northeastern Sonora, in 1760, an Opatá chief volunteered to guide him to New Mexico in a few days. The chief "knew a much shorter route than the one I planned to take via El Paso," the prelate later related.[21]

In considering the various possible routes to Sonora, Anza was acutely aware of the need for experienced guides. Precise knowledge of trails, mountain passes, and watering places was scarce. In late 1779 Anza asked Commandant General Teodoro de Croix for the services of two Sonoran soldiers, Manuel Chacón and Juan Santos Mexía. Both men had formerly served under Anza at the presidio of Tucson and had participated in the Menchero campaign in the Gila country more than thirty years before. Anza requested that they be detached and sent to New Mexico as guides for the expedition he was organizing. Investigation revealed, however, that Chacón had died and Santos had disappeared, forcing the project to proceed without their services.[22]

On November 9, 1780, Governor Anza marched out of Santa Fe with fifty presidial soldiers, plus more than a hundred citizen volunteers. He departed from his capital filled with hope that he would open the long-sought Sonora road. Commandant General Croix, who enthusiastically approved of Anza's project, had instructed military units from Carrizal in Nueva Vizcaya and the Santa Cruz presidio in Sonora to march north and attempt to support the New Mexican governor's mission. Anza's column accompanied the annual Chihuahua caravan as far as the Fray Cristóbal camp site below Socorro, separated from it and proceeded some thirteen leagues down the west bank of the Rio Grande, and then turned toward the southwest.[23]

Passing below the Mimbres Mountains in the vicinity of Cooke's

Peak, the expedition encountered a waterless *jornada* beyond the Mimbres River. Here Anza's advance sighted a trail left by forty horsemen, doubtless made by the troops from Carrizal, but he made no attempt to follow it. Probably in the vicinity of modern Deming, Anza gave up his intention of crossing the Chiricahua Mountains to the west and veered toward the southwest where springs were known to exist. This course led him down the east side of the Hatchet Mountains. On December 6 he reached the El Paso-Sonora road, and from there continued over San Luís Pass into Sonora. On December 18 Anza arrived at Arizpe, concluding a journey of 221 leagues.

Although he met friendly Gila Apaches along the way and arrived safely in Arizpe, Anza's expedition was a failure. The route he explored possessed neither the directness nor the water holes required for successful development of a wagon road. Nor had he found it expedient to join the southern support units which might have permitted a more thorough reconnaissance of the region. Commandant General Croix expressed disappointment over the results and laid plans for sending out another party the following year. This fell through, however, and nearly a decade elapsed before a serious attempt was again mounted to join New Mexico and Sonora.[24]

In 1787 Anza turned over the governorship of New Mexico to Fernando de la Concha, and returned to Sonora and assumed office as military commandant of that province and captain of the presidio of Tucson. He continued to be interested in a road to New Mexico and apparently was instrumental in dispatching an expedition in 1788 which, although dedicated primarily to punishing hostile Gila Apaches, had instructions to investigate possible highways to Santa Fe. As his age and infirmities prevented personal participation in the venture, Anza placed Don Manuel de Echeagaray, captain of the Presidio of Santa Cruz, in command. With a force of 186 men, drawn mostly from the garrisons of northern Sonora, and including Pima and Opatá auxiliaries, Echeagaray in the fall and early winter marched into the Mogollón Mountains, successfully engaged the Apaches, and advanced as far as the Zuni plains. He failed to reach the Zuni Pueblo, however, owing to a shortage of supplies.[25]

Intending to cooperate with Anza's troops, Governor Concha had led a military column from Santa Fe to Acoma Pueblo and then struggled southward across the mountains to the vicinity of the copper mines near present Silver City on the Gila headwaters. Although his scouts were unable to contact Echeagaray, Concha took several Apache prisoners and, more importantly, gained a first-hand view of the geographical barriers that hindered the cutting of a road through the region.[26]

Three years later, in 1791, Governor Concha offered suggestions to Commandant General Pedro de Nava, who was contemplating still another expedition to join the two provinces. Concha recommended that if a party were sent from Sonora to survey a road, a New Mexican company should meet it at the Gila to guide and escort it through the Navajo country. The Navajos were at peace with the Spaniards, but as a courtesy they should be advised of any major expedition passing through their domain. When asked to propose the best route, Concha replied that all he could do was to give a general delineation by direction. He reminded Nava that the major landmarks and mountain ranges were known by one name in New Mexico, by another in Sonora, and still another in Nueva Vizcaya, confusing all geographical descriptions. The governor offered to lead a detachment to link up with any expedition sent from Sonora. He warned, however, that because of the multitude of deep canyons and gorges, it would be difficult for the two parties to meet in the mountainous portion of his province. Instead, he proposed to station men on mountain peaks near the roads to both the pueblos of Zuni and Acoma and have them burn fires at night to show the Sonorans the way to these villages. But Nava's plans for an expedition did not materialize.[27]

Several years passed before another attempt was made to open the desired road. Finally in 1795, the project met a measure of success. In February of that year, Manuel de Echeagaray, who had been promoted to military commandant of Sonora, selected Don José de Zúñiga, captain of the Tucson presidio, to explore and mark a trail as far as the pueblos of western New Mexico. Zúñiga carried in his baggage a letter from his superior addressed to the missionaries and magistrates of New

Mexico. The letter enjoined them to render the captain all possible aid "in carrying out this project of opening a road to facilitate commerce and communication between the two provinces."[28]

On April 9 Zúñiga's troops, piloted by Apache scouts, departed Tucson and traveling in a northeasterly direction struck the Gila River, probably near the present Arizona-New Mexico line. Proceeding north to the Río San Francisco, they scouted the Mogollón Range, ascended through a high pass and reached Zuni on May 1. From here Zúñiga sent a letter by courier to the governor in Santa Fe, announcing his arrival and requesting that two knowledgeable men (*hombres de razón*) be detailed to return with him to his presidio and observe the trail he followed. Then, suddenly, without waiting for a reply, Zúñiga started back to Tucson, arriving there on May 29.[29]

Although Zúñiga had completed his round trip, the information he acquired added little to what was already known. His trail was too rough to negotiate by wagon, and the Apaches still loomed as a serious barrier to a regular flow of traffic. Nonetheless, General Nava soon urged that Zúñiga's route be explored further, so it could at least be of service to pack trains. Over such a route, he pointed out, a mule caravan from Tucson could reach Zuni in twenty-two days and in another fourteen be in Santa Fe. Yet his hopes were not realized. So far as is known, no additional efforts were made after 1795 by frontier officials to bridge the wilderness of southwestern New Mexico with a designated thoroughfare to Sonora.[30]

Throughout the late eighteenth and early nineteenth centuries, private groups of New Mexicans had made periodic trips to Sonora, either to trade or to conduct official business at Arizpe. In 1780, for example, a party of Santa Fe citizens journeyed to Arizpe to complain to the commandant general of certain administrative policies of Governor Anza. In this same period, caravans of merchants regularly drove carts to Sonora by way of the long road west from El Paso.[31]

Notes on this traffic were inscribed in the New Mexican governors' record of daily events (*diario de novedades*) over the years. For example, the entry on October 29, 1791, stated: "A group of citizens (*vecinos*) left this province for Sonora." On August 29, 1801, the entry included the note: "A small caravan of citizens entrusted with the mail is departing for the province of Sonora." Still another for November 19, 1803, declared: "On the 11th eighty vecinos departed heading for Sonora." And on March 30, 1804, this statement appeared: "The 16th last there arrived in this province [of New Mexico] fourteen vecinos and six Indians who had been traveling in Sonora." Later, on November 19, 1809, the governor of New Mexico informed the commandant general: "On the third of this month, ninety-one men of this province left from the village of Sevilleta headed for Sonora. I send Your Excellency a list of the goods and other things which these individuals are taking to the said province for the purpose of selling them."[32]

Curiously, some vestige of this trade persisted even after New Mexico was attached to the United States. "Up to 1859," Adolph Bandelier recorded in his journals, "regular caravans of Pueblo Indians from New Mexico visited Sonora annually, about October. Until they reached Magdalena, they were under one common head or captain. Then, they separated into three bands to trade. They had zarapes, buffalo hides, etc., and traded them for rebosos, oranges, etc. On the last day of November, the bands met at Hermosillo, and whichever did not come in until the third of December was given up for lost and all the rest left for home. In 1859, owing to an attempt at collection of duties, they never returned."[33]

Although the Spanish colonial government failed to shorten the distance to Sonora by a direct road, New Mexicans as early as the 1660s had found their way there and were taking advantage of the economic opportunities open to them. Some of the early trading parties doubtless blazed their own trails, following a route similar to that used later by Anza, or perhaps engaged Opatá guides to help pilot them between the two provinces. But these Spanish merchants kept no journals, and the extent of activities and routes of travel remain obscure. However, an investigation of available Spanish records does suggest that notwithstanding vast distances, perils of the trail, and absence of a highway, New Mexican contact with Sonora during colonial times was much greater than has been supposed.

CHAPTER EIGHT

THE RISE OF CATTLE RANCHING

In the decades prior to 1680, large landed estates, estancias, were the chief European features of the New Mexican countryside. They were essentially mixed operations, raising both livestock and crops. By the following century, ranchos, that is, small farms with a few head of stock far outnumbered the estates, now generally termed haciendas. Cattle breeding, although taking second place to sheep production, showed a steady growth from its introduction in 1598 until independence in 1821.

THE record of stock raising in New Mexico from its beginnings in the sixteenth century to the present day offers a long and fascinating story and one that figures prominently in the histories of the Hispanic and Anglo peoples who settled lands bracketing the upper Rio Grande.

Juan de Oñate introduced the first breeding stock, both cattle and sheep, when he founded the province of New Mexico in 1598. At least one of his colonists complained that the Spanish animals reproduced poorly because of the severe climate and sterility of the pasturelands. But some of the officers of the party reported just the contrary: the animals multiplied bountifully, providing abundant meat and by-products for the settlers.[1] Their claim is supported by scattered references over the next several decades that confirm that stock raising had won a firm foothold in Hispanic New Mexico.

From the outset, sheep predominated over cattle. That was in marked contrast to most of the rest of Latin America, where cattle became the major ranch livestock. Even in the neighboring Spanish provinces of Texas and California, cattle assumed first rank in the pastoral economy.

Why New Mexico should have broken with the New World pattern by giving emphasis to sheep is something that has yet to be fully explained. We know that in south Texas, cattle flourished on the inhospitable plains that were overgrown with prickly pear and were alive with predators. Turned loose to fend for themselves for much of the year, bovines developed strong feral instincts and lengthy horns for defense. Indeed, by the time Americans arrived on the scene, the rangy "long-horn cow" had evolved into a distinctive type. Cattle ranching in Texas, therefore, was something of an environmental imperative, simply because sheep were ill-suited to prosper in a land rich in six-inch cactus thorns and predators.[2]

California had neither of those problems, yet it too became

dedicated to cattle ranching. Gaspar de Portolá brought the first herd of Spanish cattle to the Franciscan missions in 1769 and Juan Bautista de Anza introduced a second as a seed herd for the colonists in 1776. So successful was this implant that by the time of the American conquest in 1846, cattle numbering in the hundreds of thousands roamed the interior valleys. It was this seemingly inexhaustible resource that made possible the booming hide and tallow trade between California ranchers and foreign merchants ships that was described by sailor Richard Henry Dana in his book *Two Years Before the Mast* (1840).

If Texas and California can be said to have followed the lead of the rest of Spanish America by turning to cattle ranching, then New Mexico elected to remain true to its Old World antecedents, for in Spain sheep dominated the herding economy and cattle were of secondary, even minor, importance. But there were also environmental factors that inclined New Mexicans toward the raising of sheep.

For one, the best pasturelands for cattle were not accessible to them during the colonial period. These were located on the High Plains along the eastern margins of the province and were carpeted with short grasses, such as gramas and buffalo grass, that cured on the stem. Here nomadic Indians held sway and, of perhaps equal significance, immense herds of bison grazed, effectively precluding establishment of a ranching industry.

The New Mexicans initiated settlement in the valleys of the Rio Grande and its tributaries, adjacent to the Indian pueblos. By the last half of the colonial period, small agricultural farms in that region came to dominate the rural landscape. Earlier, however, efforts had been made to create large-scale ranching enterprises. Before the Pueblo Revolt of 1680, these were known as *estancias*. They were stocked for the most part with a mixture of what the Spaniards called *ganado mayor* (cattle and horses) and *ganado menor* (sheep and goats).

The Franciscan missionary Father Gerónimo Zárate Salmerón wrote in 1626 that both categories of livestock were breeding well and, but for the fact that greedy governors were exporting every animal in sight to sell for personal profit, the land would be covered with them.[3] The Franciscans themselves soon got into stock raising in a large way, using Pueblo Indians to do the herding. In effect they became rivals of citizen ranchers and threw assorted roadblocks in the way of their expansion. In response, the cabildo, or town council, of Santa Fe petitioned the viceroy to force the missionaries to dispose of their cattle by distributing them to the poor. The reason given was that since the king paid the friars' salaries, they did not need the profits earned from stock sales.[4]

There was little market for either cattle or sheep in New Mexico, but demand for both was strong in the mining settlements of Nueva Vizcaya (modern Chihuahua and Durango). Mine owners had to feed their workers, and a high protein diet of meat provided the energy needed to sustain heavy labor. Also, cowhides were required to make leather ore buckets, ropes, and harnesses for draft stock, as well as shoes for the miners. And beef tallow was essential in the manufacture of candles, used to light dark shafts and tunnels. Parral, a mining center in southern Chihuahua, was a leading purchaser of New Mexican livestock sent down the Camino Real in the colonial years.

Increasingly as time wore on, that stock, driven south on the hoof, was made up mostly of sheep. We can suggest, as a second reason for New Mexico's inattention to cattle, that the presence of plentiful bison, or buffalo, close by to the east may have discouraged people from devoting efforts to that form of ranching. In other words, the annual hunts to the plains by *ciboleros* (buffalo hunters), returned huge quantities of hides, jerky, salted tongues, and tallow, much of which was exported to the mines. These products of the buffalo, free for the taking, were of a quality equal to those from domestic cattle.

The proliferation of small farms in the eighteenth century perhaps also influenced the trend away from cattle raising. Traditionally, agricultural plots in New Mexico were not fenced, so the burden of keeping livestock from trespassing fell upon the animals' owners. Sheep, as they require intensive care and handling, were easily kept away from the farmers' fields, but not so cattle, which were customarily turned loose to fend for themselves until they were rounded up for sale or slaughter.

Since cattle, for safety from Indian marauders, were grazed on the commons adjacent to the tilled plots rather than on distant pastures, the potential always existed for damage to crops. The commons were routinely overgrazed—Albuquerque's east mesa, for example, was virtually denuded of grass by 1750—so that hungry cows were drawn to the fenceless grain fields in the valleys. It was an abiding problem in all of New Spain, and laws were repeatedly passed charging owners to keep livestock under the watchful eye of herders and assigning penalties when stray animals caused harm to crops or irrigation ditches. Violations innumerable prompted constant re-passage of the laws, as in 1824, for instance, when the Provincial Deputation in Santa Fe decreed that cattle owners would have to pay damages plus a fine of two *reales* for each head of stock intruding upon farmland.[5]

One other reason can be advanced to explain the New Mexicans' preference for sheep. Throughout much of the colonial period, the province was assailed on all sides by hostile Indians, one of whose principal aims was the theft of livestock. Except for the Navajo, who had a fondness for sheep, the Indians usually went after cattle and horses, since these animals were easily and swiftly driven away. The losses to raiders are known to have been substantial. On the other hand, when sheep seemed to be in danger of seizure the herders had instructions to scatter the flock, as the owner could always recover a fair number after the raid.

The degree to which sheep outnumbered cattle fluctuated over the years, of course, but several representative figures for the late colonial and Mexican periods will convey some idea of the situation. An inventory of provincial livestock in 1779 shows 69,366 sheep versus 7,676 range cattle, a difference of almost ten to one. The disparity is reduced somewhat if we add the separate figure of 1,773 draft oxen, used in plowing and carting.[6]

A decade later, in 1787, New Mexico was able to arrange peace with the Comanches, Navajos, Utes, and Jicarilla Apaches, an event that made possible the rapid expansion of ranching. In 1791, the governor declared that because of the tranquillity in his province, "all forms of livestock were multiplying infinitely."[7] In years following, however, while sheep raising continued to mushroom, the raising of cattle not only leveled off, but actually declined. The next detailed stock census, dated 1827 (within the Mexican period), lists 240,000 sheep and only 5,000 cattle.[8] Not until well into the Territorial period would the numbers of cattle begin a precipitous climb.

A common notion long propagated by scholars is that Spain's ranching system, with its attendant traditions, served as the foundation for all American ranching. English-speaking settlers, so that theory goes, adapted wholesale Hispanic patterns of stock handling when they entered the Southwest in the nineteenth century.[9] Thus, everything from clothing, equipment, and tools to the specialized vocabulary of ranching traces back to Spanish origins.

That view has been partially challenged by cultural geographer Terry G. Jordan, who has demonstrated that Anglo emigrants entering the Spanish Borderlands actually brought with them a long heritage of open-range cattle herding that reached back to colonial South Carolina. But even he is willing to admit that a significant body of Hispanic practices and customs was soon grafted upon this heritage.[10]

Josiah Gregg, writing of New Mexico in the 1830s, gives us a vivid picture of the *vaqueros*, or local "cow-herds." He says,

> They are mounted upon swift and well-trained horses, and in the management of the animals will often perform many surprising feats . . . But the greatest display of skill and agility consists in their dextrous use of the lazo or lareat, which is usually made of horse hair.[11]

And he adds a richly detailed description of the cowboys' horse gear and clothing, which included spurs weighing two and one-half pounds and with six-inch rowels. Everything he speaks of, naturally, is in the Hispanic tradition.

In 1847, young tourist Lewis H. Garrard visited a cattle operation of Bent, St. Vrain & Company located near Cimarron on what would soon be recognized as the Maxwell Land Grant. The herders, whom he calls *rancheros*, were native New Mexicans. The foreman, or

Spanish cattle brand.

mayordomo, relates Garrard, was an intelligent-looking fellow dressed "in a blue roundabout, leather pantaloons, and peaked oil-cloth hat." The animals, he observes, were "sleek, fat, bright-spotted cattle."[12]

The reference to "spotted" is significant, for it indicates the company was running Spanish cattle—that is, the Criollo. This animal represented a native American type that emerged with the mixing of original breeds from Spain followed by adaptation to the New World environment. The Criollo is said to have run heavily to solid colors, particularly Jersey-tan and red, but spotted or piebald cows, most often black and white, were very common.[13] Inasmuch as the southern Plains Indians living adjacent to New Mexico held European bovines sacred, in the same manner as buffalo, it is not surprising that they painted spotted Spanish cattle on their shields and tepees.[14]

At least one pure breed of cattle from Spain seems to have reached New Mexico in the colonial period. Juan de Oñate, in bringing some

An example of the old breed of
Spanish cattle raised in New Mexico.

1,400 head of cows and bulls to the new land in 1598, included 100 black cattle.[15] Indeed, that was one of the requirements in his colonization contract with the king. The Black Andalusian, native to southern Spain but probably with roots in Africa, had widespread and upturned horns, a narrow face, and a draft-type conformation.[16] The last characteristic, no doubt, explains why a seed herd of black cattle was imposed upon Oñate; it was intended to furnish the draft stock for plow and cart needed in the future development of New Mexico.

References to black cattle occur throughout the Spanish Border-lands from Florida to Sonora. Herds of them were being kept by the Hopi in 1782, and others had escaped to the neighboring deserts and a feral existence.[17] By the nineteenth century black cattle, as a breed, had virtually disappeared, absorbed by the ubiquitous Criollo. The careful selection and breeding of livestock did not appear until the advent of large-scale ranching by Anglos after 1850. ∽

CHAPTER NINE

WATER THAT RUNS IN DITCHES

The vast web of irrigation ditches (acequias) seen throughout north-ern New Mexico, a system whose roots extend four hundred years into the past, represents a distinctive economic and social phenomenon without parallel anywhere else in the United States. Associated with the acequias is an accumulation of water laws tracing back to medieval Spain, and a body of customs surrounding the building and the maintenance of ditches and the equitable distribution of waters.

New Mexicans of yesteryear were in the habit of uttering a little proverb that summed up the morality of irrigation: Agua que no has de beber, déjale correr. "Water that you don't need, let it run." In other words, be frugal in consumption and leave some for the neighbors farther down the acequia. That was a wise admonition in a land of water-scarcity.

A N interesting and seldom described aspect of colonial agriculture in New Mexico is the community acequia or irrigation system used by the Spanish settlers in the upper Rio Grande basin. Irrigation practices in this area derived largely from traditional methods employed in Spain and were regulated by royal ordinances. However, since the laws allowed a measure of latitude in interpretation and application to provide local authorities some flexibility in meeting unexpected problems, and since Pueblo Indian agricultural techniques influenced, albeit to a limited degree, water uses of the colonists, the practice of irrigation in New Mexico developed along it own distinctive lines.[1]

The Spaniard's fondness for gushing fountains, whether in his patio or the public plaza, is often attributed to the perennial scarcity of water in much of his native Iberia. According to at least one author, water has been the cause of more court cases and lawsuits than has the ownership of land, and in some parts of the peninsula it represents a commodity more precious than wine.[2] Irrigation in Spain since Roman times has been employed most extensively in the arid regions of the south, particularly in Andalucía and the district surrounding Valencia. These areas were strongly influenced by seven centuries of Moorish occupation and this, together with the preponderance of words originating from Arabic that pertain to irrigation, for example, acequia (irrigation ditch), *noria* (irrigation well), *alfarda* (tax for irrigation of land), and *tahulla* (measurement of irrigated lands), has led most scholars to suggest that the practice was introduced and developed by the Moors.[3] This supposition is sometimes buttressed by reference to apparent Arabic customs associated with Spanish irrigation, such as the taking of water from acequias only after sundown.[4]

It now seems clear, however, that the processes of agriculture and irrigation used by the hardy peasants of southern Spain were known

Hoes, for directing and channeling water in the fields.

long before the Moorish invasion, and after the establishment of alien rule these old practices continued. In time a veneer of Arabic custom easily became superimposed upon traditional patterns of land and water use.[5] The Moors may have served as the vehicle by which some irrigation techniques were introduced from the East, but if that was the case, these influences must be regarded as minor accretions to the body of Spanish irrigation practice that had flourished from the days of the Romans.[6] Thus the system of irrigation brought to New Mexico at the beginning of the seventeenth century was not primarily a contribution of the Moors as has been claimed.

The journals of Spanish explorers in the Southwest often called attention to the irrigation works observed among the sedentary

Pueblo Indians. It remains uncertain how far back in prehistory these go, but probably at least as early as Pueblo III times when the Anasazi constructed terraces or check dams to retain rain and floodwaters in arroyos, and built stream diversion dams and irrigation canals.[7]

A concrete-like ditch, apparently of great antiquity, has been reported in the Sierra Blanca mountains of southeastern New Mexico and was formed when lime-impregnated water flowing from a spring to Indian fields deposited successive layers of minerals.[8] In 1883 archaeologist Adolph Bandelier discovered the same kind of irrigation ditch at a pueblo ruin near the Little Colorado River and recorded his puzzlement at viewing an acequia or concave trough that appeared to be "concrete or mexcla of some kind."[9] A similar acequia used by prehistoric farmers in the Verde Valley of central Arizona may be seen today at Montezuma Well National Monument. The most extensive irrigation system in the Southwest was that developed and used by the ancient Hohokam and their successors, the Pima and Papago, in the Gila-Salt basin of southern Arizona. Less complex, but impressive nonetheless, were the irrigation ditches at Mesa Verde in southeastern Colorado, where one canal extended a distance of four miles.[10]

Although it is freely admitted by scholars that some irrigation was practiced by the Pueblo Indians of New Mexico at the time of Spanish occupation, disagreement exists as to its intensity and kind. Antonio de Espejo, who entered the area in 1583, reported finding "many irrigated corn fields with canals and dams, built as if by the Spaniards." At Acoma he saw that "these people have their fields two leagues distant from the pueblo, near a medium-sized river, and irrigate their farms by little streams of water diverted from a marsh near the [San José] river."[11] Gaspar Castaño de Sosa, visiting San Ildefonso in 1591, noted that that pueblo had a very large area under irrigation.[12] Bandelier, investigating the old Piro district at the end of the nineteenth century, declared that these Indians had "once irrigated the bottoms along the Rio Grande, and that the number and extent of [their] fields and of the irrigating ditches connected with them, attracted the attention of the Spanish explorers at an early day."[13]

From these and other references that could be cited, it is evident that the Rio Grande Pueblos knew and practiced extensive canal irrigation at the opening of the Spanish period. At the same time, where practical, they resorted to dry farming, i.e., dependence on rainfall alone, and arroyo flood farming or utilization of land naturally flooded by arroyos, but without canals for distributing the water.[14] Owing mainly to a devastating drought that beset the Southwest at the end of the sixteenth century, dry farming and arroyo flood farming diminished in importance and canal irrigation, because of its greater dependability, came to outweigh these other methods in the Pueblo area.[15] The construction of elaborate dams and ditches and the solution of complicated problems involving the allocation of water rights were facilitated by the presence among the Rio Grande villagers of "a social organization which could mobilize and control a fairly large adult force and satisfy the irrigational needs of the society."[16] In other words, Pueblo ditches were built and managed as communal affairs, this work and the regulation of waters representing an important public task. No doubt also, the arrival of the Spaniards with their own techniques of acequia farming helped intensify the use of canal irrigation among the Pueblo Indians.

At San Juan Pueblo, where Juan de Oñate established the first settlement of Spaniards in 1598, the Indians depended largely upon rainfall for their crops, although some ditches were seen nearby.[17] According to the chronicler Gaspar Pérez de Villagrá, drought had withered the native fields so that the people came beseeching the Spanish priest to offer prayers for rain. When this was done and the sky "suddenly darkened and poured forth a regular torrent of rain, the barbarians stood spell bound in awe . . ."[18] It was well enough to trust to providence for an occasional miracle, but the colonists were wise enough to exert efforts of their own, and soon after their arrival, with the aid of the San Juan people, they began construction of acequias in order to have them ready the following spring.

The Ordinances of 1573, a set of codified instructions for the founding of new settlements, served as Oñate's guide when he laid out the villa of San Gabriel on the west bank of the Rio Grande

opposite San Juan. One article of those Ordinances enjoined coloniz-
ers to select town sites where abundant water was available for
drinking and irrigation.[19] This requirement was certainly fulfilled, but
the proximity of the villa to Indian lands in violation of other laws
may have been one of the reasons for the removal of the settlers to a
new town at Santa Fe in 1610. According to instructions delivered to
Oñate's successor, Governor Pedro de Peralta, the cabildo or municipal council of Santa Fe was empowered not only to distribute lands
but to apportion water for irrigation.[20] This was in line with long
established custom and law which accorded town councils the
responsibility of regulating and distributing water both for domestic
and agricultural use.

The first citizens of Santa Fe, probably with the aid of Mexican
Indian servants and conscripted Pueblo laborers, dug two acequias
madres (main ditches) to water fields on either side of the small river
that passed through their villa. From the canal on the north, known
after the Reconquest as the Acequia de la Muralla, a lateral ditch
brought water to the vicinity of the plaza and Governor's Palace,
although at times, it seems, a smaller acequia leading from a marsh or
ciénaga near the parish church served this area.[21] Often the flow of
the diminutive Santa Fe River was insufficient to meet the needs of
all fields, and only in wet years did farmers below the town receive
adequate water for their crops.

With the organization of other villas in New Mexico in the
eighteenth century, ample provision was made for the irrigation needs
of the settlers, although specific information on this point is scarce.
During a visit to New Mexico in 1760, Bishop Pedro Tamarón
mentioned a large irrigation ditch at El Paso of size sufficient to
receive half the waters of the Rio Grande. Subsidiary canals leading
from the principal acequia ran through broad plains to irrigate
vineyards and fields of grain.[22] The certificate for the founding of
Albuquerque in 1706 reveals that among the first tasks completed was
that of the construction of acequias "properly ditched and
running."[23] Viewing these in 1776, Fray Francisco Atanasio
Domínguez described them as being fed by the Rio Grande and so

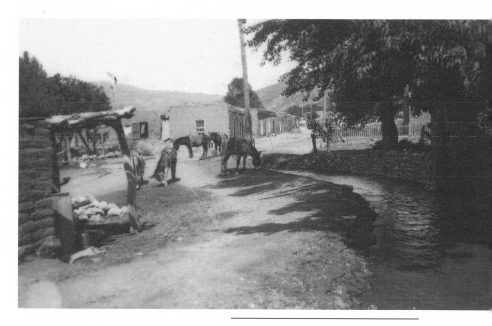

*The Santa Fe acequia madre. Open
ditches such as this were a chief
source of domestic water.*
Museum of New Mexico photograph
neg. no. 11047

wide and deep that "there are little beam bridges to cross them."[24]
The situation with regard to irrigation at the founding of another
villa, that of Santa Cruz de la Cañada in the lower Chimayó valley, was
unique among New Mexican towns. Here in 1694 Governor Diego
de Vargas forced Tano Indians to vacate villages and lands that they
had settled after the Pueblo Revolt in 1680, so that these could be
occupied by Spanish colonists coming from Mexico. Thus when the
latter arrived, they were pleased to find that the Governor had
granted them "the dwelling houses, cleared agricultural lands, drains,
irrigation ditches, and . . . dams which they said native Indians had
and did have for irrigation and the security of raising their crops."[25]

Spanish colonial law established the general principles relating to
irrigation development and its public regulation, based upon

traditional legal codes and practice in Spain. Thus the *Recopilación* provided that all the waters in the New World should be common to all inhabitants; that viceroys and other officials should supervise irrigable lands and protect them from livestock; that distribution of waters to colonists be made on the advice of municipal councils; and that whatever local provisions might be established regarding water distribution, these should be conceived so as to promote the public welfare.[26] The duties of the individual were also spelled out—water users were required to maintain and care for their acequias, to cooperate with other owners on communal ditches, and to refrain from constructing new ditches above those persons who had prior rights to the water.[27]

These laws provided a foundation upon which an irrigation system arose in colonial New Mexico, but since local demands of the environment and Indian practices helped shape this institution, attention must be given to those details that convey a picture of the distinctive situation which developed in the upper Rio Grande basin. In the first place, the community acequias were organizations composed of all landowners holding property on a ditch. They contributed labor or support in proportion to the amount of land fronting on a main acequia, whether it was cultivated or not.[28] The association of water users that had charge of an irrigation system was often one of the most highly integrated and efficient organizations in the community. This was necessary since the economic welfare, and hence the very survival of most settlers, was closely tied to the cultivation of the soil. Many of the practices directed by local associations for water distribution derived from those used in the area surrounding Valencia, Spain, where a *Tribunal de las Aguas,* managing irrigation affairs, functioned in a manner similar to the community acequias that developed in New Mexico.[29]

It should be noted that in the upper Rio Grande valley two kinds of irrigation associations appeared—the public organization and the private. The first was an adjunct of a legally formed municipality, such as the villas, or of an Indian pueblo. In these the acequia madre was regarded as public property and its management was the responsibility of the municipal government. The private organization was one formed in a community that had limited or no legal status and lacked a town government. By far the largest number of New Mexican colonists lived in small rural hamlets of this kind. Here the community ditches were voluntary undertakings on the part of interested water users. Although there was no intervention or direction by a municipal council, strict regulation was provided by an elected mayordomo or ditch boss.[30]

So little information is available that the manner in which the four colonial villas in New Mexico superintended their irrigation systems is not clear. There exists a single reference to an *alcalde de aguas* in the villa of El Paso in 1802,[31] who may have been analogous to a *juez de aguas* or water inspector found in other parts of Spanish America.[32] If such an officer existed in the remaining New Mexican villas, he perhaps functioned in place of a mayordomo.[33] In rural districts it is certain that the alcalde mayores exercised some jurisdiction over irrigation matters, especially with regard to formal complaints or suits involving damage to ditches by livestock or theft of waters.[34]

Concerning the duties and activities of the mayordomo who oversaw management of ditches in New Mexican villages and in the Indian pueblos, a good deal is known, particularly since the office continues today and many time-honored practices dating from the Spanish period have been preserved. Originally, under call and direction of the district alcalde, male members of a community acequia gathered annually to elect a mayordomo, or in some instances two or three, and to determine the amount of his salary. Once selected, the ditch boss enjoyed a large measure of authority and prestige. He inspected and superintended repair of acequias, regulated the number of days' labor required of each proprietor, distributed and apportioned water, adjudicated disputes, and searched for infractions of regulations.[35] From the mid-nineteenth century there remains at least one formal list, probably prepared by the mayordomo, of proprietors along the new ditch of Chamisal near Belen, which carefully tabulates acequia frontage and days of labor owed by each man.[36] Because of widespread illiteracy and scarcity of

Log flume (canoa) *for carrying of
irrigation water over an arroyo,
near Las Trampas.*

paper during the colonial years, it is doubtful if such written records
were common under the Spanish regime.

The amount of irrigable land cultivated by a single farmer
averaged only ten acres in the 1850s, and this had probably long been
the case. Larger farms were concentrated in the Río Abajo below
Santa Fe where the floodplain of the Rio Grande widened, but above
the capital valleys were narrow and discontinuous along the main river
and its tributaries, limiting the amount of cropland available to each
family.[37] The pattern known for the Chama valley in the late eighteenth century was perhaps typical of remote areas in the northern
district. Here agriculture was practiced little above the subsistence
level because the men and older boys devoted the bulk of their time
to the care of livestock, hunting, trading and militia service. After
clearing a section of bottomland and digging acequias for irrigation,

they left the raising of crops to women, children, and the elderly, who used a digging stick rather than the plow.[38]

The construction of a new irrigation system required the expenditure of a considerable amount of labor on the part of the settlers. Diversion dams and acequias were modeled to some degree after those used in Mexico and Spain, but owing to the lack of surveying instruments, heavy tools, and engineering skills, the works here were simpler and less efficient. For example, in testing the fall of an acequia under construction, water had to be turned into it frequently to observe the amount of grade since no surveyor was available. Furthermore, ditches were seldom straight, their builders zig-zagging around trees, boulders, small hills, and other obstructions.

The first problem to be considered was that of obtaining a head of water copious enough to supply a new ditch. Usually a river or stream was tapped two to four miles above farmlands, so that by gravity flow the water could be carried through the acequia madre to smaller canals leading directly to the fields. On the Rio Grande, with its abundant volume and low banks, a diversion wing of stones was often sufficient to turn the current into a canal.[39] Elsewhere, on small or intermittent streams where a ready source of water at the right level was lacking, recourse was had to dams (*presas*) to impound the flow and form a reservoir that might be conveniently tapped.[40]

By all accounts the New Mexican dams were crude affairs of logs, brush, and stones easily destroyed by spring freshets or summer flash floods. The one at El Paso in 1773 was described by a local citizen as "made of wattles, as the terrain of the river does not permit any other kind of fabrication, to say nothing of the trouble caused by its excessive floods and freshets, for it not seldom happened that after a dam had been built of stones, fagots, and stakes, it was necessary to tear it down in order to prevent inundation of the town."[41] A traditional-style dam seen by James W. Abert near the village of Manzano in 1846 was "very large, constructed of crib-work, 12 feet wide, and 8 feet high, and 100 feet long, formed of rough logs, and the interior filled up with stones and earth."[42] On dams of this nature little or no provision was made for diversion, so that the structure had to carry the weight and pressure of whatever quantity of water descended from above. If the pressure was too great and the dam was lost, crops might perish from lack of water before it could be replaced and normal flow restored to the acequias.[43]

The construction of ditches below the point of diversion from the main stream was undertaken by the collective manpower of the community. Primitive hoes and shovels of wood served in the absence of iron tools during colonial days, and earth was removed on rawhides pulled by oxen.[44] Main acequias averaged from three to five yards wide and from two to six feet deep.[45] Earth thrown out of the ditch each spring as it was cleaned soon formed a mound several feet high and helped stabilize the bank. The acequia madre was always kept above the land to be irrigated so that waters could be released into the lateral or secondary channels and carried to the fields below. These secondary ditches, called *brazales* in Spain, were known in New Mexico as *contra acequias*, or more commonly during the colonial period as *sangrías*.[46] Headgates of wood admitted water from the acequia madre into the lateral channels, and as soon as the flow reached his field the farmer with a hoe made small dams "so as to overflow a section at a time . . . depressing eminences and filling sinks, and causing the water to spread regularly over the surface."[47] Working in this slow and tedious way, a cultivator could irrigate five to six acres in a day.

When water was plentiful, users might draw whatever quantity they wished from the ditches.[48] In times of scarcity, however, the supply was strictly rationed by the mayordomo who supplied permits to take water for a limited time. In such cases a farmer frequently kept his entire family working all night irrigating his patches of ground. Especially during a drought, quarrels and serious conflicts over water allotment were common. Some of these ended in court and others with bloodshed.[49] A related problem is illustrated by the text of an alcalde's decree in 1813:

> Those who must irrigate by bringing water from up above another ditch, should construct a flume (*canoa*) wherever the waters cross, so that owners of the other ditches will not be harmed and to avoid theft of waters which might otherwise

be made under the pretext of emptying water from one irrigation ditch to another. In such an event, other parties would be denied the benefit of their own work and would lack water they need, so that their crops would be held back and damaged. And he who does not build a flume when he should, must pay the consequences, suffering four days of imprisonment in the public jail.[50]

An important aspect of the development of Spanish irrigation in New Mexico concerns the influence it exerted over traditional systems of the Indians. Apparently many of the community irrigation customs of the Pueblos were entirely compatible with Spanish institutions and were allowed to continue. This was in conformity with laws set forth in the *Recopilación* that provided that ancient customs of the Indians should be retained and respected so far as practicable.[51] Nevertheless, it is apparent that Spanish practices, such as organization of labor under a mayordomo and techniques of dam and acequia construction were gradually adopted by the Pueblos. They continued to retain, however, ancient ceremonial practices surrounding irrigation, such as the planting of prayer sticks in the ditches and ritual dances following cleaning of the acequias in spring.

With Indians and Spaniards often living side by side, there were numerous instances of joint use of acequias. Serious controversies over the method of administering such ditches arose not infrequently, with the district alcalde acting as arbiter to settle matters in dispute.[52] Along the Rio Grande near El Paso in the 1770s, the mission Indians and colonists were living commingled, "the former having their farms and a branch irrigating ditch, while the latter have the main ditch, containing two flood gates from which the Indians' water comes. The upkeep of the dam is obligatory upon all."[53]

Another source of friction was unattended livestock that wandered onto Indian land, not only stripping fields but damaging irrigation ditches. Soft, sandy banks along canals easily collapsed under the hooves of grazing stock, filling the ditches or causing breaks that permitted escape of precious waters. From the first introduction of horses and cattle into New Spain, the royal government repeatedly passed legislation designed to safeguard Indian farm plots, but the laws were generally ignored.

One of the earliest of these in New Mexico was a decree of 1620, which ordered that large stock of the Spaniards be kept at least three leagues distant from the pueblos and Indian fields.[54] Again in 1687, the governor of New Mexico issued a proclamation requiring stockmen to keep their animals out of growing crops and away from irrigation ditches.[55] When the Indians of San Juan Pueblo complained in 1718 that their fields and acequias were suffering grave damage from cattle owned by residents of the villa of Santa Cruz, the lieutenant governor in Santa Fe prohibited the latter from leaving their livestock unattended.[56] A century later the alcalde of the Jemez jurisdiction announced:

> In vain have the superior authorities demanded compliance with orders which prohibit grazing-stock from being pastured alongside cultivated fields or along the banks of irrigation ditches . . . If the Indians should suffer serious damage, severe penalties will be imposed on transgressors . . . Whenever loose animals are found in fields, the owner must suffer the fine of one-half a real of silver for each head.[57]

Even such strict measures as this seemingly had little effect, mainly because fencing of cropland and ditches was not practiced and stockmen continued to be careless about providing a herder for their animals. Withal, it is plain that for Indian as well as Spaniard, maintaining and protecting an irrigation system on the New Mexico frontier was a vexatious but necessary task.

CHAPTER TEN

SAINT JOHN'S DAY, REMNANT
OF AN ANCIENT FESTIVAL

*While pieces of traditional Hispanic culture, such as the irrigation
system and some folk arts, have survived into modern times, much else
has been lost and almost forgotten. The once popular feast day of St.
John the Baptist, for instance, has now given up nearly all of its old
secular entertainments and customs that formerly ranked it as one of
the most keenly anticipated festivals of the summer season. A review
of the main activities that defined St. John's Day in New Mexico can
convey to us something of the flavor of the original folk culture.*

A T the beginning of the final week of June 1846, itinerant Irish artist Alfred S. Waugh reached New Mexico's capital with a wagon train from the East. "The day we entered Santa Fe," he wrote, "was the festival of St. John, or Midsummer's Day, and the whole town was alive with mirth and jollity; business seemed to be suspended, and the inhabitants gave themselves up to amusements of all sorts with a perfect abandonment of rational feeling."[1]

The annual cycle of religious festivals coinciding with the rhythm of the seasons was one of the distinctive features of traditional Hispanic life along the upper Rio Grande. Perhaps the most popular of summer observances was the feast of San Juan (June 24), honoring St. John the Baptist. "In every Spanish village the greatest concentration of old customs and superstitions occurs on Midsummer Day."[2] The author of that statement was speaking specifically of Spain. But he just as well could have been referring to New Mexico. In a similar vein, Charles F. Lummis, after personal observation in the 1890s, affirmed that the Día de San Juan in nearly every pueblo and New Mexican hamlet is marked by celebration.[3]

Anglo-Americans of the nineteenth century, who encountered this eventful day, usually missed its historical and religious significance and reported only the details of one spectacular aspect of the occasion, the *corrida de gallo*, or rooster pull. That was the case with Santa Fe trader Josiah Gregg, writing of the 1830s, and territorial secretary William W. H. Davis, in the mid 1850s.[4] Even Lou Sage Batchen, collecting folklore in 1939 from old-timers in Las Placitas and Ojo de La Casa, focused at length on a memorable corrida that took place on June 24, 1888, without mentioning the religious side of the day's happenings.[5] None of these authors, nor the majority of others dealing with the subject, ever makes reference, like Waugh, to the connection between Midsummer's Day and the Día de San Juan.

This celebration furnishes a useful case study of the way a popular

European religious devotion—the honoring of a saint on his feast day—evolved and took on distinctive characteristics among the rustic frontiersmen of Spain's remote province of New Mexico. It also offers an example of the blending of Indian and Old World ritual elements that contributed, through four hundred years of history, to the emergence of a unique folk culture in upper New Mexico.

In pre-Christian Europe, Midsummer's Day falling near the solstice was associated with renewal, fertility, magic and unrestrained merrymaking. Across Europe, including Spain, bonfires blazed in streets and plazas and on neighboring hilltops on Midsummer's Eve (June 23). People danced around them and as the flames subsided, they leaped over the fires believing they thereby gained protection the rest of the year from sickness and misfortune.

In ancient Rome, Midsummer's Day traditionally saw a raucous festival dedicated to lovers (fertility) and to purification by fire and water. Underlying the lighting of bonfires was the widespread notion that fire served as an agent to guarantee a plentiful supply of sunshine for agriculture. Conversely, water, particularly bathing, played a conspicuous part in Midsummer's rites, since washing one's self on that day functioned as a rain-charm.[6]

As primitive Christianity spread across the continent, it actively sought to capture and tame the pagan rituals and customs so beloved by the masses of common folk. In the process, the festival of Midsummer's Day was re-dedicated to the feast of the nativity of St. John the Baptist (San Juan Bautista). Not only was he among the most honored saints of the early Church, but because of his identification with the sacrament of baptism, he came to be regarded as the patron of the purity of water, which became pure on his day, June 24.[7]

In tribal societies around the world, the shedding of human blood was often linked to rain-making ceremonies. That St. John was martyred by bloody beheading may have reinforced in the popular mind his connection to water and rain. In any event, many of the paganistic rites and beliefs that had characterized the old Midsummer's Day festival persisted into the Christian era and were assimilated, somewhat grudgingly, by the Church. As a consequence, the keeping of St.

John's Day exhibited a mixture of the sacred and profane.

Nowhere was that more evident than in medieval and modern Spain. There, on his day, San Juan was thought to cast his blessing over all things on earth, but most notably he blessed the waters, giving them miraculous properties. Women before sunrise went to bathe in the streams, or alternatively washed their faces and arms in the village fountain. In the province of Navarre, young girls disrobed and rolled in the dewy grass. Such symbolic cleansing was supposed to promote good health. With that in mind, farmers in some regions drove their livestock to the rivers for bathing.[8]

The bonfires of antiquity remained much in evidence on San Juan's Eve, with children dancing around and leaping over them. In the Pyrenees Mountains, youths descended from the heights carrying pitch-pine torches. Formerly, cloth dummies representing the old spirit of vegetation were burned on Midsummer's Eve, but with the Christianizing of the festival this particular activity was identified as "burning Judas."[9] It is clear, therefore, that water and fire, as deeply rooted symbols of renewal, continued to play a conspicuous role in the Church's celebration of the Día de San Juan.

Adding to the constellation of practices associated with this day in Spain are several amatory or fertility customs. Marriageable girls, for instance, attempted to learn the identity of their future husbands by breaking a raw egg in water and looking for his face to appear in the yolk. At sundown on June 24, country lads would serenade their favorite maidens, then decorate their windows and balconies with flowers and tree boughs. On the following afternoon, young couples went to the fields, taking baskets of *roscas*, a heavy ceremonial bread baked in the shape of a ring, to eat with white cheese.[10]

Another custom led elderly women to go out and pick medicinal herbs between midnight and dawn of San Juan's Day. The plants were considered, during that brief interval, to be unusually potent and thus efficacious in the curing of all illnesses. The harvested herbs might be left on the ground until morning so that a coating of dew could enhance their power.[11]

Apart from the religious and magical aspects of the occasion, the

Día de San Juan afforded an opportunity for revelry, representing the secular side of the Church holiday. Besides parades, dancing, and singing, the brutal sports of bullbaiting (*corrida de toros*) and cockbaiting (corrida de gallos) were also common diversions. The origins of both are quite obscure because they are so ancient. The fighting of bulls, however, was familiar to Spain's first inhabitants, the Iberians, whose descendants taught the Romans. Those Iberians also had a bull cult, which probably meant that the fights and blood-spilling carried religious significance. When the Moors invaded Spain in the eighth century, they too became fervent patrons of bullfighting.[12]

Cockbaiting, known to the ancient Greeks and Romans long before the Christian era began, continued to be widely practiced in the Middle Ages. In eastern cultures, the chicken traditionally had ritual-istic uses. The Jews, for example, once considered it a sacrificial animal. The baiting of cocks took a variety of forms, the best known being the cockfight in which a pair of roosters fought to the death in a shallow pit (*arena de gallos*) surrounded by betting spectators.[13]

Another form of cockbaiting involved the suspending of a rooster by its feet from a rope stretched about thirty feet above the ground. Horsemen in turn galloped under the rope, rose in their stirrups, and in passing attempted to wring off the bird's head. The feat was made more difficult because at the crucial moment of contact the rope was jerked upward, by men on either end. As a variation, the rooster could be buried in the ground with only its head and neck projecting. Riders dashed by and leaning from the saddle tried to grab the small, bobbing target. Finally, if horses were unavailable, young people were blindfolded, spun about, and then pushed in the direction of the cock hanging from a rope. They thrashed wildly in the air with a wooden stick until the bird was reduced to tatters.[14]

Spanish harvest festivals, fairs, and the most solemn religious holi-days routinely included corridas, inasmuch as a passion for them was shared by all social classes. A bullfight, for instance, was held to honor the canonization of St. Theresa of Avila. The Church banned cock-fighting as early as 1260 but the prohibition was universally ignored.

Josiah Gregg. In his Commerce of the Prairies *(1844), he gave one of the earliest descriptions of Spanish rooster pulling.*
Museum of New Mexico photograph neg. no. 9896

When Pope Pius V issued an edict in 1567 threatening bullfight participants with excommunication, Philip II, with support of the Spanish bishops, declared that his nation would disregard the papal pronouncement. By that time, bull and rooster corridas were already widespread throughout the Spanish Empire, along with the familiar celebration of the feast of San Juan Bautista.[15]

In the colonial Viceroyalty of New Spain, which included the province of New Mexico on its far northern frontier, the June 24 festival devoted to St. John flourished in both cities and rural communities. As in Spain, considerable variation existed from one region to another in the particular celebrative customs observed. However, a standard schedule of core events was widely accepted and followed. Among them were preliminary functions on St. John's Eve, water renewal rites at dawn of the 24th, succeeded by church services and a procession, and concluding with an afternoon and evening of assorted amusements and merry-making, cockbaiting being conspicuous.

When New Mexico's founder, Juan de Oñate, ascended the Rio Grande with his colonizing expedition in 1598, he named a small Piro pueblo in the Socorro district, San Juan Bautista, because he passed the night there on St. John's Eve. June 24, we also presume, was his personal saint's day. Capitan Gaspar Pérez de Villagrá declares that Oñate ordered a holiday to celebrate the occasion, the centerpiece of which was the staging of a sham battle. In the Captain's words, "The horsemen skillfully clashed in combat, showing great dexterity in the handling of their arms." So far as is known, this was the first formal commemoration of the feast of St. John in New Mexico.[16]

Regrettably, further references to this celebration are so thin that little can be said about its configuration during the more than two centuries of the colonial period. Not until American merchants arrived on the scene, after Mexican independence in 1821, do descriptions with some detail finally become available. Among those, as noted, was Josiah Gregg who was perhaps the first writer to provide an account of a New Mexican corrida de gallo on the festival of San Juan.[17]

The importance of the day in traditional New Mexican culture is emphasized by the local custom of identifying June as *el mes de San Juan* (the month of St. John), just as July was termed the month of St. James (Santiago) whose feast fell on July 24.[18] A further measure of San Juan's status can be drawn from reference to his popularity in the religious folk art produced by provincial santeros. The fact that his festival coincided with the beginning of New Mexico's rainy season lent extraordinary weight to an ecclesiastical holiday already closely associated with water and rain-making. In the arid land of New Mexico, rain in early summer was essential to supplement the irrigation waters that were starting to grow short after the spring run-off of snow melt. Behind outward events marking the day, therefore, one finds symbolic elements of renewal, purification, fertility, and *machismo*.

The picture drawn here, based on the latter-day accounts of New Mexico's San Juan observance, represents a variety of practices and customs reported in Indian as well as Hispano communities. The Pueblo people in assimilating Spanish Catholicism tended to "Indianize" many elements of public ritual and performance. Moreover, since they had a long tradition of religious conservatism, their distinctive celebrations survived intact into the twentieth century for a longer time than was the case among the Hispanic population.

St. John's Eve events are poorly recorded, perhaps because they seldom attracted the attention of visitors. An exception was the tourist couple Carl and Lilian Eickemeyer, who described the San Juan celebration in 1894 at Cochiti Pueblo south of Santa Fe. At sundown of the 23rd, the church bell began incessant clanging, with hourly pauses to allow the shooting of guns into the air. According to the Eickemeyers, "this alternate ringing and firing, together with violin-playing by some [New] Mexicans who wandered through the plaza, making noisy demonstrations all the while, ushered in San Juan's Day."[19]

Anthropologist Charles H. Lange was on hand for the occasion in 1947 and indicated that little had changed since the Eickemeyers' day. But in addition to the bell-ringing and gunfire, he saw fireworks and bonfires.[20] In fact, all four things had originally been characteristic of public celebrations in general. U.S. road commissioner George C. Sibley, for example, while in Santa Fe on a secular holiday in 1825 viewed "bonfires lighted throughout the city."[21]

While it is safe to say that bonfires (*hogueras*) were once commonplace in New Mexican towns and villages on San Juan's Eve (Lange's observation of them at Cochiti in 1947 representing a vestigial survival), it is less clear whether in the minds of local people there remained any memory of the significance of Midsummer Eve fires in Spain. No reports, for instance, have surfaced of celebrants along the Rio Grande dancing around their hogueras, or leaping over them for good luck.[22]

Nor have we yet found mention of women gathering herbs on St. John's Eve, or young men serenading their favorite maidens, as was the widespread custom in Spain. One folk practice remembered by native scholar Aurelio M. Espinosa, however, had a direct parallel in

*A village celebration with
traditional bonfires, Galisteo,
New Mexico.*
Museum of New Mexico photograph
neg. no. 133005

the Mother Country. In New Mexico, he wrote, "On the eve of St. John's Day the white of an egg was placed in a glass of water, and the next morning what is to happen in the future appears written on the egg."[23]

In both New Mexico and Spain, bathing or washing took place at dawn, to obtain the benefits of purified waters and also to engage in an imitative ritual of the sacrament of baptism. The custom in late nineteenth-century Arroyo Hondo, north of Taos, was recalled long afterward by Cleofas M. Jaramillo:

> The women of the village were up early on the twenty-fourth
> of June. At six o'clock they were bathing in the river or in the
> acequias. Later in the morning the small children were seen
> also in the river and ditches . . . for on this day the waters in
> the streams were believed to be holy. Better health awaited
> those who rose early to bathe at least their faces and feet in
> the holy water. For was it not St. John who baptized Jesus in
> the river Jordan and blessed the waters?[24]

Concha Ortiz y Pino de Kleven, age 89, states (1999) that when
she was a girl at Galisteo, the older village women went down to the
river at sunup for ceremonial bathing. At the same time, they would
also cut their hair, for what reason she could not remember.[25] An
explanation of the practice, however, is provided by Espinosa: "On St.
John's Day women cut the tip of their hair with an axe, or simply
wash it, so that it may grow."[26] The same tradition exists in the
countryside of central Mexico where girls ask a male relative to lop off
ends of their hair with a machete on San Juan Day, to make it grow.[27]
Encouraging new hair growth fit in with the renewal theme of the
holiday, but that the cutting might be done with an ax or machete
points directly to symbolism surrounding the beheaded San Juan
Bautista.

In New Mexico's Pecos Valley, people named Juan or Juana
(called collectively "Juanes") were sometimes rebaptized in the river
on their saint's day, a more specific commemoration than the general
bathing.[28] Going to the streams or irrigation ditches at dawn must
have been fairly universal in the old society, but by the time folkways
became a subject for formal study, it had lapsed in many Hispanic
communities. An interesting variant is reported in the mid-twentieth
century from the Nambé Valley. Here, young people were strictly
prohibited from wading or bathing in the acequias or the local pond
until the day *after* June 24, that is, after the priest at Mass had blessed
the waters on the Día de San Juan.[29]

There is no evidence of "dawn bathing" among the Pueblos, but
at Cochiti occurred a curious custom whose origins are obscure. In
the afternoon, following the usual corrida de gallos, families having a

member named Juan or Juana carried gifts of food, cloth, hides, pottery and so forth to the flat rooftops, along with large containers of water. Villagers moved in a crowd from house to house, and at each one the gifts were thrown to upraised hands. Sometimes recipients struggled for possession. Simultaneously, the water was flung in an arc so that participants below received a good showering. Other Pueblo towns, among them Zia and Acoma, throw gifts but drenching of the crowd is missing. Whether Cochiti's custom comes from the association of San Juan with water and baptism, or whether it derives from the familiar Indian practice of inducing rain through resort to sympathetic magic has not been determined.[30] Hispanics are apt to call up an old folk saying when it rains on June 24: "San Juan is crying, but they are good tears."[31]

The centerpiece of the day's religious observances was Mass in the village church, provided a priest was available. The service often included a special blessing of the waters, as at Nambé, which would have particularly appealed to the desert-dwelling New Mexicans. If a community had no resident clergyman and could not obtain one from a neighboring town, then a morning lay-service was conducted by the church mayordomo. This official was appointed annually by the parish priest to collect contributions from the parishioners, and also direct religious functions at which a priest was not required to officiate. On San Juan's Day, the mayordomo led his congregation in prayers, hymns, and sometimes in recitation of the rosary.[32]

Following Mass or the lay-service, some sort of procession might be staged, its nature varying from one place to another. Arroyo Hondo enjoyed one of the most elaborate processions, at least according to available accounts. Participants carried outside an image of Our Lady of the Rosary, attired for the occasion in a blue silk dress, where she was mounted on a wooden platform under a canopy of white muslin. Borne by four men, she occupied a place of honor at the head of the cavalcade. Behind her, a single man walked with a statue of San Juan Bautista in his arms. Other santos from the church were also carried.

Arroyo Hondo is an attenuated community, stretching almost three miles along its stream course. As the procession moved slowly down the valley, a boy in the lead beat a small Spanish drum (*caja*) steadily, tom-tom fashion, to announce their approach. Backing him up were a half dozen young men discharging old-style muskets at intervals along the way. As they neared the first residence, the tempo of the drum increased and the muskets thundered in unison. The lady of the house emerged holding a plate of live coals. Upon these she sprinkled incense or sugar and perfumed the statues with a cloud of aromatic smoke. Kneeling in front of the virgin, she kissed the hem of her dress, then carried the image into her *sala*, or front parlor, followed by the bearers of the other statues.

There a home altar had been erected, decorated with candles, wild flowers, and evergreen branches. The santos were placed upon it, and all who could crowd into the room knelt, sang hymns, and prayed. Afterward, the procession re-formed and continued to the next house where the reception and ritual were repeated. An extended excursion was made through the fields, too, so that the prolonged event lasted till dusk. In conclusion, a wake (*velorio*) in honor of the saints was held throughout the night in the last house. Observer Reyes N. Martínez remarked that the strange thing about all this was that in Arroyo Hondo "St. John took second place to the Virgin Mary."[33]

Elsewhere, the procession generally was much shorter in duration and less elaborate. At San Mateo, for example, following Mass all the congregation would simply process through the few streets, accompanied by their statue of St. John and singing traditional hymns.[34] The women of neighboring San Rafael, by contrast, took their image of San Juan to the fields at dawn for a special blessing.[35]

In Galisteo during the early twentieth century, it was customary for the mayordomo (Tomasito Peña) to ring the bell summoning the town's people to church. There he led them in reciting El Rosario. Instead of a procession, a kind of mobile chorus then formed, composed mainly of women and children. This group walked to the houses of the Juanes to honor them on their saint's day, in part by singing in the street the Spanish hymn, "El Día de San Juan." Words of the song were reminiscent of a quatrain recited in Andalucia on St. John's Day.[36]

Isleta Pueblo, downriver from Albuquerque, produced its own distinctive ritual—a mix of Indian and Hispanic elements—for the morning observances. As soon as the Franciscan padre had finished with Mass, village boys carried a red banner of San Juan in procession from the church three times around town and into the pueblo's extensive fields. Upon returning from the fields, they brought new cornstalks and deposited them at the church. Next, they visited the homes of Juans and Juanas, who gave them live roosters, bread and goat cheeses. The first rooster collected was taken to the church and placed on the altar for the priest, while the remainder were reserved for the pending corrida de gallo.[37] In all instances, both Indian and Hispanic, in which a village's San Juan image was paraded through the fields, it can be interpreted as a supplication to him for a bountiful rainy season.

Once the morning procession was completed by New Mexicans, the rest of the day was given over to amusements, or as Waugh at Santa Fe put it in 1845, to "mirth and jollity."[38] In late morning or early afternoon, musicians with guitar, violin and sometimes a drum might walk through the community playing and singing an invitation to a dance to be held in the evening. This musical advertisement was referred to as *tocar el gallo*, or "playing the rooster." Oddly, the term gallo (rooster) was applied to several different types of events. The Indians at Cochiti, for instance, have always referred to their gift- and water-throwing simply as *gallo*. Presumably, this usage comes from the fact that in the entertainment line, the corrida de gallo was the defining event of the day, and thus lesser activities took the name gallo because of their association with it.[39]

In midday there was much visiting from house to house, especially those where Juanes lived. Relatives came from other communities, and people dwelling on isolated farms and ranches arrived to partake of the available religious and social opportunities. Every family prepared a special noon meal that might include such local Spanish delicacies as mutton roast and *arroz con leche* or *sopa* for dessert.[40] No visitor went hungry.

As preamble to the much anticipated corrida, or rooster pull, villagers turned out to walk in a Spanish-style promenade or ride horseback in the dusty streets. For a saint's day, young and old dressed in their best finery, even if for a poor girl that meant no more than wearing a new ribbon in her hair. Anglo newcomers were initially surprised to observe that the local folk got dressed up for these festivals, while on the other hand they came to Sunday church in their everyday work clothes.[41] Waugh watched men, women, and boys on June 24 riding in the capital's plaza "jostling and tilting against each other." And he adds, "Many Señoras gaudily dressed sat behind the gentleman and enjoyed the fun as much as anybody."[42] Gaily attired couples on a single horse can still be seen in Spain today on certain holidays.

The corrida de gallo quite likely was part of New Mexican folk culture from the days of earliest settlement. However, the first documentary reference to a corrida dates from 1689 when soldiers at El Paso (that place then being within the jurisdiction of New Mexico) competed in a rooster pull in front of the *casas reales*, or government buildings. Much betting on the results occurred, a practice that would persist up to modern times.[43]

Gregg referred to the New Mexicans' passion for cockfighting, and bullfights were held, at least in Santa Fe, on important religious and secular occasions in the colonial period and as late as 1844.[44] But neither one became identified locally with San Juan Day, as happened in Spain. Instead, the popular corrida de gallo took hold on the Rio Grande and became the star attraction during the afternoon's entertainment.

It should be emphasized that rooster pulls in New Mexico traditionally formed part of a number of summer saint's day celebrations, notable among them being San Pedro (June 29), Santiago (July 24), and Santa Ana (July 26). Nevertheless, as Lummis suggested in 1891, the corrida on San Juan's Day remained the preeminent one.[45]

The reasons, already noted, were 1) the Saint's connection with water and rain-making; and 2) the symbolic parallel between the beheading of St. John and decapitation of the rooster. How much conscious recognition of the latter existed among New Mexico's

Hispanics and Pueblos is open to question. But anthropologist Elsie Clews Parsons states that among Guatemalan Indians "the rooster pull of San Juan Day is associated conceptually with the beheading of the saint."[46] It is difficult to believe that the convergence was not obvious to the New Mexicans as well.

A proper corrida de gallo required advance preparation. During the week prior to the Día de San Juan, *los galleros* (the rooster pullers) grain-fed and groomed their horses, while exercising them to bring their mounts to peak condition. In some places, the roosters to be sacrificed were collected ahead of time and held in readiness. The local *patrón* might donate the birds, or occasionally it would be the rural alcalde (magistrate), as at Agua Fría, where he served as the director of the corrida. Often in both Hispanic and Indian communities, those persons named for the saint were obligated to donate a rooster as an offering. At Las Placitas, each adult named Juan was visited by the galleros, on horseback, on the morning of the corrida. He gave them a rooster or, lacking one, he forfeited a silver coin.[47]

As in Spain, the rooster was "pulled" by New Mexicans in two different ways—either buried in the ground with his head and neck protruding or suspended by his feet from an overhead rope or from a tree. "In either case," notes Gregg, "the racers passing at full speed, grapple the head of the fowl." And he adds that the head "being well-greased, generally slips out of their fingers."[48] In the first instance, the rooster's feet were tied together and he was buried in a shallow pit, with the dirt loosely packed. In the second, he was hanged by his feet from an overhead rope, just barely within reach of the rider, and tied in such a way as to permit the entire bird to be jerked free with a single tug. In reality, that was the aim of the gallero, but not surprisingly sometimes when the dirt was packed too tightly or the tie to the over-head rope was made incorrectly, the victim could lose his head prematurely. As many as a dozen roosters might be used up in a single corrida.

In the nineteenth century, there was a tendency for Hispanics to bury the rooster, while the Pueblos hanged him from a rope. But in fact, the two peoples on occasion used both methods.[49] As a rule,

*Navajo Indian burying a rooster in
the sand, in preparation for a "pull."*
Museum of New Mexico photograph neg.
no. 21671

corridas de gallo were open to all participants. Santo Domingo
Indians pulled roosters at Hispanic Galisteo and also, for a time, at
neighboring Cochiti Pueblo. Navajos took part in "pulls" at the
western pueblos and at Spanish towns like San Mateo where they
were welcomed.[50] At a few conservative pueblos, such as Santo
Domingo and Acoma, however, New Mexicans were generally
excluded, perhaps because the event in those places had become
largely absorbed by the native religion.

The Hispanic villagers often formed teams of galleros that would
challenge teams from other places. Longstanding rivalries and betting

on the outcome produced heated encounters. In preparation for the event, an experienced gallero lengthened the stirrup on the side he intended to make his pass. With his horse at a run, he would lean down with all his weight in that stirrup while hanging on to the horn, saddle strings, or mane. Men with long arms and legs were thought to enjoy a natural advantage.[51] Still, catching the bobbing head of the rooster involved as much luck as skill.

The riders assembled en masse some distance from the buried fowl. The director of the corrida designated the order in which men would make their dash upon the bird. He signaled when each could begin by shouting *al gallo* or by firing a shot in the air. The rider took his turn and upon missing the grab, another immediately followed him. The difficulty of the feat ordinarily ensured that considerable time elapsed before someone plucked the rooster from his "living grave." When that occurred, the entire body of riders descended upon the victor. His team mates, or if there were no formal teams, then his friends encircled him to run interference. The successful gallero shouted a challenge to his rivals, all of whom were attempting to snatch the prize from his hands. Still holding the bird by the head and neck, he swung it in the air like a club and belabored his foes. It was at this point that the beheading was most apt to occur.[52]

Breaking free of the pack, the victor raced out into the open country, hotly pursued by the dare-devil throng. Anyone who caught him reached for a wing or leg, and in the grappling, *el gallo* was dismembered. If the gallero was fortunate enough to return with a recognizable portion of the corpse, he waded into the crowd of spectators and, according to Gregg, "presents it to his mistress, who takes it to the fandango which usually follows, as a testimony of the prowess of her lover."[53]

In Gregg's statement can be discerned the element of *machismo*, or super manliness, that colored participation in the corrida de gallo. Folklorist Arthur L. Campa remarked that youths who succeeded at pulling roosters were regarded as *muy hombre*, very manly, and their proud fathers boasted and beamed. A triumphant gallero earned the accolade of community hero.[54] The intensity of the event, as Lt.

Bourke observed in 1881, allowed "the display [of] some exception-
ally fine feats of horsemanship."[55] And in frontier society, riding skills
counted heavily in defining "a real man."

Notwithstanding, in New Mexico at least, those same skills were
admired in women. They also took part in a corrida de gallo, not on
St. John's Day but on St. Ann's day, July 26. That leads us to believe
that the true underlying motive of rooster pulling was to honor a
particular saint, and only secondarily to flaunt one's manhood or
womanhood by a demonstration of riding proficiency.[56] In any event,
by the early twentieth century, women were abandoning the role of
gallera because "it was too cruel to appeal to them."[57] Instead, they
merely got dressed up and rode horseback through the plaza and
streets. The last reference to galleras in a corrida was at the little
village of Agua Zarca (San Miguel County) in the early 1940s.[58]

During the final decades of the nineteenth century, the corrida de
gallo became more violent and dangerous. An increased spirit of
competition led to more falls from horses, resulting in serious injuries
and occasional deaths. Lt. Bourke described them as accidents, yet
some of the casualties were caused by fights. Lummis proclaimed that
the Pueblo Indians almost never lost their tempers, but in mad
scrambles for the rooster, the New Mexicans "seldom finish without
bad blood, and frequently not without bloodshed."[59]

The physical hazards faced by the galleros, the bloody tearing apart
of the rooster, the heavy betting, and atmosphere of wild abandon
seemed more in keeping with pagan celebrations of antiquity than with
Christian commemoration of a saint's day. Indeed, one searches in vain
for specific acknowledgment by Hispanic participants that rooster
pulling had any religious significance of its own. By contrast, the
Pueblo Indians were plainly aware of the supernatural link.

To them, the splashing of rooster blood during the fight for
possession had the magical power to summon the life-giving rains.
The red droplets anointed the backs and shoulders of the galleros. A
religious cacique at Acoma blandly informed an anthropologist that
the "blood of the rooster is good for rain."[60] Strict custom at Santo
Domingo forbade cleaning the sweat and lather from a horse's back

following the corrida. The Indian explanation furnishes a vivid example of sympathetic magic, with sweat symbolizing rain and lather, clouds: "When the horses and men get sweaty, that is a prayer to God and Rey [King] for rain."[61] Another instance of such magic is provided by Acoma galleros, who, following the corrida, went among the exhausted horses in the corral, filled their mouths with water from little jars, and sprayed it over their favorite mounts.[62] Frazer points out that among a number of Indian tribes, a ritual could be found in which water was sprayed from the mouth in an imitation of a mist or drizzling rain.[63]

The pulling of roosters was widely regarded as a sport or game, an activity that, in the Hispanic sector at least, helped establish the Día de San Juan as a "fun day" as much as it was a religious holiday. Universally, the occasion concluded with an evening dance, called a fandango in Gregg's time, but by the early twentieth century commonly referred to as the *baile,* a softer and more polite term. The etiquette and customs associated with that dance were the traditional ones that had prevailed in New Mexico for generations. In some places, bonfires were lit, as on the previous evening. Those at Galisteo were kindled in front of the house of the Juanes.[64]

World War II, which saw up-rooting of families and re-orientation of the rural economy, sounded the death-knell for much of New Mexico's traditional folk culture that had survived since the colonial era. By midcentury, even Pueblo elders were lamenting that the young no longer knew how to do religious things properly, and did not even seem to care. As far as San Juan Day was concerned, the cluster of customs marking the festival had been diminishing for fifty years, and such things as ritual bathing and cutting of the hair, processions to the fields, and serenading the Juanes were things of the past. The bailes continued longer, but they too were eventually abandoned, leaving only a vestigial religious service in the village church.

The period from 1900 through the 1950s also witnessed the decline and extinction of the corrida de gallo in Hispanic communities, although it survived in several Indian pueblos into the twenty-first century. The loss could be attributed to a number of causes: a growing distaste for the barbarity of the "sport," a new unwillingness to suffer the injuries and fatalities, the increasing scarcity of riding horses and the ebbing of superior horsemanship the old corridas required, the difficulty in procuring sacrificial roosters, and finally a general loss of interest in "out-dated" entertainments.

Young people of today have little or no knowledge of the corrida de gallo or of the once rich tradition of celebrating the Día de San Juan on the Rio Grande. The festival whose antecedents reached far back into antiquity has run its course. ◈

CHAPTER ELEVEN

THE SPANISH EXILES

Mexico's break with Spain in 1821 was not cleanly made, for after ten years of bitter struggle, the royal government in Madrid was still unwilling to acknowledge the de facto separation. Thus for the remainder of the decade, the Empire's threat to renew hostilities kept relations in a precarious state. Caught in the middle were native-born Spaniards who had long resided in Mexico.

D URING 1828 and 1829, a handful of New Mexico residents were expelled from the country by order of the Republic of Mexico. They were *peninsulares*—persons born in Spain, that is, on the Iberian peninsula—and the stern action taken against them was based on politics, patriotism, and matters of international diplomacy. The story of these Spanish New Mexicans, made refugees against their will, has never been examined in detail. But a look at the background and the unfolding of the episode reveals a curious sidelight on our history.

By the Treaty of Córdoba, signed August 24, 1821, the last viceroy of New Spain, Juan O'Donojú, recognized Mexican independence. That treaty, however, was repudiated by Spain. During the following decade, the royal government made several abortive attempts to recover its lost colony. The constant threat of invasion by Spain kept Mexican officials on edge and finally led them, in the latter 1820s, to take retaliatory measures against native-born Spaniards who had remained in the nation unmolested since independence.[1]

The first in a series of legislative decrees, passed May 11, 1826, proclaimed that Mexico would entertain no formal relations with Spain until the latter recognized Mexican independence. And it added that any resident of the nation who spoke out against such recognition would be declared a traitor and subject to capital punishment.[2]

One year later (May 10, 1827), a new decree prohibited Spaniards from holding civil, military, or ecclesiastical office until such time as Spain extended recognition to Mexico.[3] That measure produced severe social dislocations since numerous military officers and the majority of the clergy were from Spain.[4] But worse was to come.

A decree of twenty-one articles, dated December 20, 1827, provided for a partial expulsion of Spaniards living within the Republic.[5] The term partial is usually applied because the act made provisions for numerous exemptions. For example, persons married

16

PROHIBICIÓN A LOS ESPAÑOLES PARA OBTENER EMPLEOS

(MAYO 10 DE 1827)

1. Ningun individuo que sea español por nacimiento podrá ejercer cargo ni empleo alguno de nombramiento de los poderes generales en cualquier ramo de la administracion pública, civil y militar, hasta que la España reconozca la independencia de la nacion.

2. Se estiende lo prevenido en el artículo anterior á los cargos y empleos eclesiásticos del clero secular y regular, en cuanto al ejercicio de sus atribuciones económicas, gubernativas y judiciales. Esta disposicion no comprende á los reverendos obispos.

3. El gobierno queda autorizado para separar hasta por el tiempo de que habla el artículo 1º á los curas, á los misioneros y doctrineros del Distrito y Territorios de la federacion.

4. Tampoco se comprenden en los artículos anteriores los hijos de mexicanos que casualmente nacieron en la península y se hallan en la República.

5. Los empleados que se separen del servicio en virtud de esta ley, gozarán todos sus sueldos, y se les abonará el tiempo en sus carreras respectivas.

6. Los empleos vacantes por las disposiciones que contiene esta ley, se desempeñarán provisionalmente conforme á las leyes.

7. Los curas que separare el gobierno en uso de las facultades que le concede el artículo 3º, continuarán percibiendo todos sus emolumentos en los mismos términos que antes de su separacion; y los coadjutores ó substitutos serán pagados de la hacienda pública.—Cárlos Garcia, presidente de la cámara de diputados.—Tomás Vargas, presidente del senado.—Vicente Güido de Güido, diputado secretario.—José Antonio Quintero, senador secretario.

Por tanto etc.—A D. Tomás Salgado.

Decree prohibiting Spaniards from holding office in *Relaciones diplomáticas: México-España (1821–1977)*.

Order expelling Spaniards.

to Mexican nationals were exempt, as were individuals over the age of sixty and those with a physical handicap. More sweeping was Article 7, which allowed Spaniards to remain who had given distinguished service to the cause of independence and who, subsequently, displayed their devotion to the Republic's institutions. Spaniards not exempt—and that included pointed mention of the regular clergy—were required to depart in six months.

On the whole this initial order of expulsion must be considered as mild, particularly when we remember that it was passed in an atmosphere of crisis, amid growing signs that Spain intended to take military action against the nation. Clearly, the decree of December 20 was aimed at preventing internal subversion—one article, for instance, prohibited exempt Spaniards from living along the seacoast where invasion was expected. Notwithstanding, it is apparent that the majority of those who were ultimately expelled offered no real threat to Mexico's security. They may have derived some solace, however, from another provision in the decree that allowed their return to Mexico as soon as Spain extended recognition.

In New Mexico, as in other parts of the country, local authorities took steps to enforce both of the 1827 decrees against Spaniards. The exact number of Spanish-born persons living in the territory then is unknown, but it appears to have been something over a dozen. Of those, as many as one-third may have been members of the clergy.

Through much of the colonial period, a majority of the missionary friars serving in New Mexico were natives of Spain. A census of 1789 for the *Custodia de San Pablo del Nuevo México,* for example, shows that fifteen of a total of twenty-four resident priests were Spanish-born.[6] While the number of clergy significantly declined in the waning colonial years and during the first years of independence, at least six of those remaining on duty in New Mexico during the late 1820s traced their birthplace to the Mother Country.[7]

In the summer of 1827, Governor Manuel Armijo at Santa Fe (then exercising his office under the title *jefe político*) received a copy of the national decree of May 10—the one forbidding Spaniards from holding public office. He referred the document to the *diputación territorial*, that is, the legislative assembly, which served him as an advisory council. Apparently no immediate action was taken to remove Spanish priests from their posts, as the new decree mandated, probably because no Mexican replacements were available. But the diputación did inform Armijo that it had recently initiated proceedings against the Spaniard Manuel Echevarría, teacher of a private school in Santa Fe. His school was ordered closed on charges that he had violated the law and was guilty of cruelty to children.[8]

By early the following year, 1828, Armijo had in his hands a copy of the first expulsion decree, issued the previous December 20. His initial targets were five Spanish Franciscans, namely:

Fr. José de Castro, age sixty, a native of Galicia, arrived in America in 1795, reached New Mexico in 1802, currently the priest at Santa Clara Pueblo.

Fr. Teodoro Alcina, age sixty-one, a native of Gerona in Cataluña, reached Mexico in 1792 and continued on to New Mexico, arriving there in March 1793.

Fr. Juan Caballero Toril, age fifty-five, a native of the province of Córdova, served in New Mexico eighteen years, currently the priest at San Miguel del Vado.

Fr. Antonio Cacho, age forty-four, native of Castilla la Vieja, reached Mexico in 1819, served at the missions of Jemez, Zia, and Santa Ana.

Fr. Manuel Martínez, age forty-one, native of Castilla la Vieja, reached Mexico in 1819, currently the priest at San José de la Laguna.

Under the decree, the governor was empowered to exempt from expulsion those priests who met certain provisions of the new law. Castro and Alcina, for example, were permitted to remain because they were sixty years of age or over. Each man subsequently took an oath before Armijo and other witnesses, swearing recognition of Mexican independence and promising to defend the nation and government from all enemies.[9]

The three remaining Franciscans also wished to stay, claiming exemptions because they had demonstrated "affection for independence" and had served the nation by continuing to labor as missionaries.

They underscored the last point by mentioning that the government salary (*sínodos*) due them had not been forthcoming over the past eight or nine years, and, as a result, they were reduced to poverty. Father Caballero tried to strengthen his claim by reference to a persistent ailment that had afflicted him for the past nine years. He stated that a long trip into exile might prove fatal.[10]

Governor Armijo, however, was unyielding and ordered Fathers Caballero, Cacho, and Martínez to depart New Mexico by the next March 13 (1828). They were allowed by law to select the port from which they wished to exit the country, and all three chose the Tamaulipas port of Soto la Marina on the Gulf of Mexico. They were also entitled to travel funds, but since by Armijo's own admission his treasury was "extremely short," the governor could provide money sufficient to see the exiles only as far as El Paso del Norte. He did append notes to their travel papers, however, asking officials in El Paso, Chihuahua, and Monterrey—towns along the route to Soto la Marina—to furnish aid so that the missionaries could continue to the coast.[11]

At the same time that he was prosecuting the case of the clergymen, Armijo took action against several other Spaniards then residing in New Mexico. Manuel Echevarría, the disgraced teacher, was directed to leave Santa Fe on March 9 for Taos, where presumably he could join the next party of Americans heading for the United States.[12] Later in 1828, however, he appeared in Chihuahua and asked the authorities to reexamine his case.[13]

Another Spaniard expelled from New Mexico at this time was Benito Bengochea whose exit papers show that he was expected to leave the country by way of Durango, Mexico City, and the port of Veracruz.[14] Instead, he fled to Sonora where, according to a report received by Armijo, he was receiving shipments of arms at Guaymas, probably in anticipation of a Spanish invasion.[15]

Seventy-three year old Antonio Pérez, a native of Santander, who had been a property owner in New Mexico for twenty-eight years, won a reprieve, because of his advanced age, and was allowed to take a loyalty oath.[16] The Spaniard Atanacio Bolíbar, a resident of Santa Fe, however, got only a three-month delay in his sentence of expulsion. Governor Armijo allowed him to remain in the capital until June 9 to collect debts that were owed to him.[17] Later in the year, an Antonio Bolívar of Santa Fe appeared in Chihuahua where he petitioned the authorities to permit him to remain.[18]

During succeeding months, the governor turned up several more Spanish-born persons. Among them was Fr. Manuel Bellido, who arrived in New Mexico about 1820, and was now serving the Indians of Picuris Pueblo. He was sent to Mexico City, and there he asked the government for 500 pesos, as travel money and as remuneration for his eight years of missionary work in New Mexico.[19] Two other Spanish laymen, Antonio Jiménez and Francisco Galis, received exemptions from Armijo and were allowed to stay.[20]

Some writers have claimed that those Spaniards who escaped expulsion in New Mexico did so by the payment of bribes. L. Bradford Prince, for example, declared that the friars "Albino [*sic*] and Castro were permitted to remain on account of their advanced age—*and* the payment of $500 each! It is not believed that any large portion of this sum reached the official treasury."[21] Ralph Emerson Twitchell repeats the charge of the friars' paying a bribe and adds that the money went to two leading officials of the territory. "The motive was one of avarice and not of charity," he writes. "It may be safely stated that very few Spanish-born residents of New Mexico would have left the territory had they been provided with sufficient funds to satisfy the demands of the officials."[22]

Neither author cites a source for these charges, and, indeed, they must have been based on hearsay since unscrupulous officials are not in the habit of leaving a documentary record of their bribes. Available documentation strongly suggests that Armijo and members of his government carefully followed the letter of the law, exempting five persons and exiling at least six others. There is no proof, of course, that bribery did not intrude on occasion, but that the two destitute friars were forced to pay $500 each, as Prince and Twitchell contend, seems highly unlikely.

More than a year after promulgation of the first decree of expulsion, a second and far more severe decree was issued, March 20, 1829. It was prompted by new rumors of a Spanish invasion, rumors that proved all too true. The following July, a Spanish army of three thousand troops sailed from Havana and briefly captured the Gulf port of Tampico. During the panic preceding that event, the central government concluded that for patriotic and security reasons, Spaniards who had escaped expulsion earlier should now be banished. Stern penalties were provided for those who failed to comply with the order.

For those exiles who could not afford passage out of the country, the March 20 decree provided that their expenses, "with the strictest economy," be met by the public treasury. And each was to be given a ship ticket to the nearest port in the United States.[23] In fact, of the more than 1,400 Spaniards expelled in 1829, some 70 percent sailed to New Orleans. They were mainly poor merchants, shopkeepers, and laborers, who hoped that peace would soon be established allowing them to return. Wealthier Spaniards, for the most part, took ship for Cuba or Europe.[24]

As a result of the new decree, two of New Mexico's Spaniards, who earlier had been exempted from expulsion, were now ordered to leave. They were Antonio Pérez and Francisco Galis. Another so treated was a recent arrival by way of the United States, merchant Manuel Alvarez, who would later return to Santa Fe as the U.S. consul.[25]

As harsh as the new policy was, New Mexican authorities were able to exempt the aging priests Castro and Alcina and the layman Antonio Jiménez (or Ximenes), all being permanently disabled. Further, Fr. Manuel Vineres, a Spanish missionary exiled from Sonora, was given permission to stay in New Mexico while he submitted documents to Mexico City seeking an exemption for health reasons.[26]

The action taken against Spaniards on the upper Rio Grande was repeated throughout the Republic. By early summer of 1829, for instance, the state of Chihuahua had provided for the expulsion of some seventy-five persons, including a priest and a layman at El Paso del Norte. A special commission for public security set up by the state legislature formulated a decree, subsequently enacted, which spelled out stiff penalties for Spanish residents failing to leave and fixed a time limit of twenty-five days for Spaniards, exiled from other states, to cross Chihuahua on their way out of the country.[27]

Americans watched the unfolding of this chapter of Mexican history with undisguised interest and no little sympathy for the largely innocent Spaniards abruptly separated from their homes and businesses. *Niles' Register* of Baltimore, sometimes called the *Time* magazine of its day, referred in March 1829 to Mexico's pending expulsion decree. "We had hoped that the peace and security of the country would not have required the adoption of so severe a measure—and one that must deprive the republic of a large portion of its enterprise and capital."[28] Later, when the full text of the Mexican law was received, the *Register* acidly labeled it "a cruel decree . . . unworthy of the age in which we live." And the paper blamed the act on partisan politicians who "were ready to sacrifice every principal of right to the possession of power, and reckless of the misery of other men."[29]

In the months following the expulsion decree of March 20, the American press carried frequent notices about Spanish refugees leaving Mexico and arriving in the United States. Most of the exiles, as indicated, went to New Orleans by ship. But one small group chose to travel overland from New Mexico via the Santa Fe Trail.

In early June 1829 the annual trading caravan from Missouri had departed for Santa Fe. Because of recent Indian hostilities, it was escorted by Major Bennet Riley and troops of the 6th Infantry from Fort Leavenworth. The soldiers went only as far as Chouteau's Island, a noted trail landmark in southwestern Kansas, because at that point the merchant train crossed the Arkansas River into Mexican territory. After a harrowing trip, beset by Indian attacks, the caravan reached Santa Fe.

Concluding a summer's trading, the merchants started their return about September 1. Major Riley and his men, encamped for the season at Chouteau's Island, awaited their arrival so as to provide an escort for the second half of the eastward journey. But the real danger lay on the first leg, in Mexican territory. Col. José Antonio Viscarra, inspector-general of the Mexican troops at Santa Fe, volunteered to assemble men and provide protection as far as the American boundary.

At that time, a group of Spanish exiles was looking for means to reach the United States. With the added security offered by Colonel Viscarra and his seventy or so regulars and militiamen, the Spaniards decided to chance a crossing of the prairies with the caravan. Milton Bryan, one of the Missouri traders, spoke long afterward in his memoirs of "the disloyal Spaniards who were banished." He wrote: "When we started on our homeward journey, seven priests and a number of wealthy families, comfortably fixed in wagons more like our railway coaches than ordinary wagons, accompanied us."[30]

Mexican records give the number of exiles as ten men accompanied by six women, the latter presumably wives or other relatives.[31] Unfortunately, no reference is made to names or place of origin. Possibly one or more of the three Spanish residents of New Mexico, ordered out in 1829, were numbered among the group. However, the majority, if not all, of the exiles must have been from Chihuahua or other north Mexican provinces. They would have ridden to Santa Fe during the spring and summer, hoping to find passage with eastbound Americans.

The caravan's return proved as harrowing as its outward journey. The company sustained a major Indian attack near the Cimarron River but managed to fight its way to the rendezvous with Colonel Riley by October 12. There, during a two-day layover, Riley and Viscarra entertained one another with formal dinners. In his official report, Colonel Riley refers to the exiles among the new arrivals as, "one Spanish family [and] eight or ten other Spaniards, who were punished by their laws for having been born in old Spain. . . ."[32] A junior officer, Lt. Philip St. George Cooke, observed "a large number of grave Spaniards, exiled from Mexico, and on their way to the United States, with much property in stock and gold—their whole equipage Spanish."[33]

After taking leave of Colonel Viscarra, Riley escorted the caravan as far as eastern Kansas where, being out of the danger zone, he left the wagons and guided his men back to Fort Leavenworth. The caravan broke up before crossing into Missouri, one portion continuing on to the head of the trail at Franklin in the central part of the state.

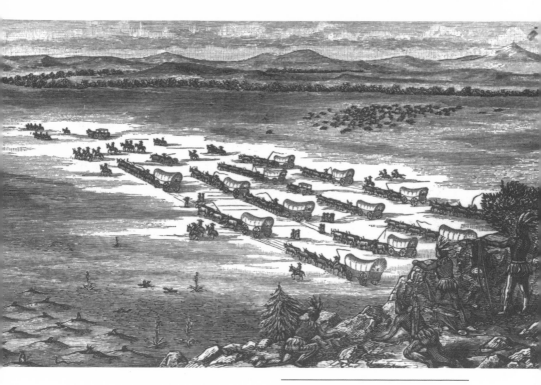

*In an American caravan such as
this the Spanish exiles traveled to
Missouri.*
Museum of New Mexico photograph
neg. no. 87450

On November 1, the *Missouri Intelligencer* (located at Fayette, a few miles north of Franklin) took note of the returning train from Santa Fe. "From fifteen to twenty of our citizens . . . have just reached their homes in good health and spirits. . . . Accompanying the traders are several Spanish families of the class who were expelled from the Mexican republic . . . and who have chosen a refuge and home among us."[34]

How many of the exiles may have remained on the Missouri frontier and how many others continued on to St. Louis or perhaps New Orleans is not known. The Spanish priests certainly would not have lingered among the mainly Protestant, backwoods folk. A year and a half later, one party of Spaniards, whose sentence of expulsion evidently was lifted, started back to New Mexico. Trader Josiah Gregg, who embarked for Santa Fe with wagons in May 1831, related: "Those who accompanied us [included] members of a Spanish family who had been banished in 1829, in pursuance of a decree of the Mexican congress, and were now returning to their homes in consequence of a suspension of the decree."[35]

The social and economic impact that the expulsion decrees had upon Mexico cannot be fully measured. At the very least, it can be said that hundreds of families were uprooted (and in some cases split apart), businesses were ruined, a large amount of capital wealth was removed from the country by the exiles, and severe strains were placed on the church through loss of clergy.

Effects of the decrees were less injurious to New Mexico owing to the small number of Spaniards resident there. But even so, their influence can be noted. The church, whose ranks were already badly depleted, must have felt keenly the loss of four priests. Before departing, the Franciscans, it can be mentioned, turned over their sacred vessels, vestments, statues, paintings, and "a library of various volumes," to Domingo Fernández of Santa Fe (a member of the Third Order to St. Francis) for safekeeping.[36]

Another effect of the decrees, and the patriotic rhetoric that accompanied them, was to promote prejudice against all Spaniards among the Mexican populace. As late as 1846, wandering artist Alfred S. Waugh learned from Manuel Alvarez, who had returned to Santa Fe as U.S. consul, that Spaniards "are even more obnoxious to the Mexicans than are Americans; on one or two occasions, the mob here have attempted his life."[37] Seeds of social discord, once sown, are difficult to root out.

Perhaps the most accurate and succinct judgment came from Mexico's great conservative statesman Lucas Alamán, who characterized the entire expulsion episode as, "a very grievous spectacle."[38] Those words applied as much to New Mexico as to the rest of the Republic. ❧

INTRODUCTION

1. George P. Hammond and Agapito Rey, eds. and trans., *Don Juan de Oñate, Colonizer of New Mexico, 1595–1628*, 2 vols. (Albuquerque: University of New Mexico Press, 1953), 1: 199–308.

2. Hammond and Rey, *Don Juan de Oñate*, 1: 522–30.

3. The complete list is included in the contract translated in France V. Scholes, "The Supply Service of the New Mexican Missions in the Seventeenth Century," *New Mexico Historical Review (NMHR)* 5 (January 1930): 93–115.

4. On the abuse of Indian labor during the administration of the notorious Governor Bernardo López de Mendizábal, 1659–61, see France V. Scholes, *Troublous Times in New Mexico, 1659–1670*, Historical Society of New Mexico, Publications in History (Albuquerque: University of New Mexico Press, 1942), 47–50.

5. Ovidio Casado, "Don Francisco Cuerbo y Valdés, Governor of New Mexico: 1705–1707" (master's thesis, University of New Mexico, 1965), 26.

6. Hubert Howe Bancroft, *History of Arizona and New Mexico, 1530–1888* (San Francisco: The History Company, Publishers, 1889), 279.

7. Donald Jackson, ed., *The Journals of Zebulon Montgomery Pike*, 2 vols. (Norman: University of Oklahoma Press, 1966), 2: 50.

8. Petition of Albuquerque citizens, 22 May 1974, Spanish Archives of New Mexico, Series II, Document number 454, New Mexico State Records Center and Archives (SRCA), Santa Fe. Hereafter, these documents will be cited as SANM, with proper series and document number.

9. Virginia L. Olmsted, trans. and comp., *Spanish and Mexican Colonial Censuses of New Mexico, 1790, 1823, 1845* (Albuquerque: New Mexico Genealogical Society, 1975), 1–14.

10. Governor's economic report, Santa Fe, 1803, SANM, II, no. 1670à.

11. For an example, see Marc Simmons and Frank Turley, *Southwestern Colonial Ironwork* (Santa Fe: Museum of New Mexico Press, 1980), 32.

12. Concha to Ugarte, Santa Fe, 20 June 1788, Archivo General de la Nación, Mexico City, Provincias Internas, 161.

13. Marc Simmons, ed. and trans., *Father Juan Agustín de Morfí's Account of Disorders in New Mexico, 1778* (Isleta, N.Mex.: Historical Society of New Mexico, 1977), 12.

14. Charles Wilson Hackett, ed., *Historical Documents Relating to New Mexico, Nueva Vizcaya, and Approaches Thereto, to 1773*, 3 vols. (Washington, D.C.: Carnegie Institution, 1923–1927), 3: 468.

15. Proceedings against Diego de Torres, 13 April 1735, SANM, II, no. 402.

16. Bancroft, *History of Arizona and New Mexico*, 249.

17. Bernardo de Gálvez, *Instructions for Governing the Interior Provinces of New Spain, 1786* (Berkeley, Calif.: Quivira Society, 1951), 42.

18. Simmons, *Morfí's Account*, 19.

19. Luís Navarro García, *Las Provincias Internas en el Siglo XIX* (Sevilla: Escuela de Estudios Hispano-Americanos, 1965), 13n.

20. Manuel Carrera Stampa, "Las Ferias Novohispanas," *Historía Mexicana* 2 (1953): 319–42.

21. The best source on the Jalapa fair is José J. Real, *Las Ferias de Jalapa* (Sevilla: Escuela de Estudios Hispano-Americanos, 1959). For a sketch of the Acapulco fair, see Vito Alessio Robles, *Acapulco en la Historía y en la Leyenda* (Mexico: Porrúa, 1948), 123–35.

22. H. Bailey Carroll and J. Villasana Haggard, eds. and trans., *Three New Mexico Chronicles* (Albuquerque: Quivira Society, 1942), 36.

23. Order of Governor Cruzat y Góngora, 12 October 1732, SANM, II, no. 377.

24. Orders and Decrees, II, 115, a supplement to SANM. See also Max L. Moorhead, *New Mexico's Royal Road* (Norman: University of Oklahoma Press, 1958), 43.

25. Carroll and Haggard, *Three New Mexico Chronicles*, 106.

CHAPTER ONE

1. *Popé* was the most frequent spelling of the Pueblo Revolt leader's name in the original Spanish documents, and for that reason it is spelled that way still by most historians. However, modern Indian writers appear to prefer *Popay*, or *Po'pay*.

CHAPTER TWO

1. Hackett, *Historical Documents Relating to New Mexico*, 3: 327–35.

2. James J. Burke, *This Miserable Kingdom* (Santa Fe: privately printed, 1973), 129.

3. Américo Castro, *The Spaniards, an Introduction to Their History* (Berkeley: University of California Press, 1971), 583.

4. Ramón Menéndez Pidal, *The Spaniards in Their History* (New York: W. W. Norton, 1966), 18.

5. William Lytle Schurz, *This New World* (New York: E. P. Dutton, 1964), 81.

6. Troy S. Floyd, *The Bourbon Reformers and Spanish Civilization* (Boston: D. C. Heath, 1966), 18.

7. Nettie Lee Benson, ed., *Report of Dr. Miguel Ramos Arizpe* (Austin: University of Texas Press, 1950), 40, 24, 19.

8. Dennis E. Berge, ed., *The Mexican Republic, 1847* (El Paso: Texas Western Press, 1975), 24.

9. Ovidio Casado, *Don Francisco Cuerbo y Valdés* (Oviedo, Spain: Instituto de Estudios Asturianos, 1983), 26.

10. Eleanor B. Adams, ed. and trans., *Bishop Tamarón's Visitation of New Mexico, 1760* (Albuquerque: Historical Society of New Mexico, 1954), 104.

11. Hackett, *Historical Documents Relating to New Mexico*, 3: 157.

12. SANM, II, no. 2625.

13. Karl A. Wittfogel and Ester Goldfrank, "Some Aspects of Pueblo Mythology and Society," *Journal of American Folklore* 56 (Jan.–Mar. 1943): 16–30.

14. Florence Hawley, Michael Pijoan, and C. A. Elkin, "An Inquiry Into Food Economy and Body Economy at Zia Pueblo," *American Anthropologist* 45 (Oct.–Dec. 1943): 547–56.

15. *Autos Sobre Quejos de los Religiosos Franciscanos* (Mexico: Editor Vargas Rea, 1947), 36.

16. SANM, II, no. 793.

17. Ibid., no. 2012.

18. Ibid., no. 899.

19. Cunningham Transcripts, Library of Congress, Box 280. From Secretaría de Guerra y Marina, Archivo General de la Nación, Mexico, legajos 1787–1807.

CHAPTER 3

1. Hackett, *Historical Documents Relating to New Mexico*, 3: 379.

2. A Spanish facsimile of the original document of certification, together with an English translation, is provided by Lansing B. Bloom, ed., "Albuquerque and Galisteo, Certificate of Their Founding, 1706," *NMHR* 10 (January 1935): 48–50.

3. *Recopilación de Leyes de los Reynos de las Indias*, 4 vols. (1681; reprint ed., Madrid: Ediciones Cultura Hispánica, 1973), book IV, title V, law 6; and book IV, title VII, laws 1–12. The requirement of thirty families to found a villa was not a rigid one. San Antonio, Texas, was organized as a villa in 1731 with only sixteen families—Canary Islanders enlisted by the king to colonize New Spain's frontier. The enterprise was carefully superintended by the viceroy, and his instructions to the governor of Texas gave precise details as to the manner of forming a plaza, streets, residential lots, and commons. The viceroy also provided a map, *plano de la población*, to serve as a guide for forming the new villa. Lota M. Spell, ed. and trans., "The Grant and First Survey of the City of San Antonio," *Southwestern Historical Quarterly* 66 (July 1962): 73–89.

4. The Spanish use of an extra "r" in Albuquerque was dropped, through Anglo-American usage during the first half of the nineteenth century. An article in the *Rio Abajo Weekly Press*, 7 July 1863, contending that Albuquerque with a single "r" was the correct spelling in Spain, is erroneous.

5. Archivo General de la Nación, México, Provincias Internas, legajo 38, expediente 8 (AGN); and Richard E. Greenleaf, "The Founding of Albuquerque, 1706: An Historical-Legal Problem," *NMHR* 39 (January 1964): 9–10.

6. Greenleaf, "The Founding of Albuquerque," 10.

7. Petition, 8 March 1892, Records of the Court of Private Land Claims, SRCA, Microfilm Roll 34. In this file see also the Plat of the City of Albuquerque Grant, showing the "imagined four square leagues."

8. Greenleaf, 1–15; and Applicant's Brief, no. 70800, District Court Records of Bernalillo County, Albuquerque.

9. Hubert Howe Bancroft, *History of Arizona and New Mexico, 1530–1888* (1889; reprint ed., Albuquerque: Horn and Wallace Publishers, 1962), 221; and Ovidio Casado, "Don Francisco Cuerbo y Valdés, Governor of New Mexico: 1705–1707, His Career and Personality" (master's thesis, University of New Mexico, 1965), 24. The alternate spellings, "Cuervo" and "Cuerbo" are both used in the contemporary documents.

10. Prior to the reconquest, New Mexico governors were appointed by the viceroy. But beginning with the term of Vargas, they received their appointments directly from the king. The viceroy then could make only provisional, or interim, appointments when a governor died in office or resigned. Ted J. Warner, "Don Félix Martínez and the Santa Fe Presidio, 1693–1730," *NMHR* 45 (October 1970): 271.

11. "Méritos de Cuervo, con memorial y suplico. . . ." Mexico, 6 October 1712, in Archivo General de las Indias (AGI), Guadalajara, leg. 116, part 2. See also Casado, "Don Francisco Cuerbo y Valdés," 1–4.

12. Casado, "Don Francisco Cuerbo y Valdés," 26.

13. Ralph Twitchell, *Spanish Archives of New Mexico* (SANM), 2 vols. (Cedar Rapids, Iowa: The Torch Press, 1914), 2: no. 110; *Autos* and muster roll, Santa Fe, April 1705, SRCA.

14. Casado, 42.

15. John L. Kessell, *Kiva, Cross, and Crown* (Washington, D.C.: National Park Service, 1979), 303.

16. "Certification of the Santa Fe Cabildo," 23 February 1706, AGI, Guadalajara, leg. 116, part 2.

17. "Inventory of the Archives of the Cabildo of Santa Fe, 1715," SANM, I, no. 1136. This grant and similar ones in the Middle Valley were probably not occupied until late 1705 or 1706.

18. Hackett, *Historical Documents Relating to New Mexico*, 3: 375; Isidro Armijo, trans., "Information Communicated by Juan Candelaria, Resident of This Villa de San Francisco Xavier de Alburquerque Born 1692—Age 84," *NMHR* 4 (July 1929): 276.

19. Richard E. Greenleaf, "Atrisco and Las Ciruelas, 1722–1769," *NMHR* 42 (January 1967): 6.

20. See, for example, Peter Gallagher, "The Founding of Albuquerque," *Rio Grande History* 7 (1977): 2–5; and Fray Angélico Chávez, "The Albuquerque Story," *New Mexico Magazine* 34 (January 1956): 18–19.

21. Ralph E. Twitchell, *Spanish Colonization in New Mexico in the Oñate and De Vargas Periods* (Santa Fe: Historical Society of New Mexico, 1919), 21.

22. That Captain Martín Hurtado, rather than Governor Cuervo, carried out the actual founding of Albuquerque is confirmed by a land grant document of 9 March 1707, addressed to Hurtado as alcalde mayor of the villa. It reads: "Lorenzo de Carabajal, a resident of this town of Albuquerque and San Javier, appears before you and asking that all privileges allowed by law be given him, says that . . . on the seventeenth day of the past year of 1706, the alcalde mayor assigned to me and gave me possession of the ruins of an old house which had belonged to my father [before the revolt], and you were also pleased to set off to me a small piece of farm land on the day that you made the partition of the lands of this villa to the citizens and new settlers by virtue of the royal authority which was given you for that purpose and other purposes. . . ." Signed: Lorenzo de Carabajal. SANM, I, no. 156.

   The founding date of February 7 is given by Juan Candelaria. However, the reliability of this and other statements of his concerning early Albuquerque has been questioned by Chávez, "The Albuquerque Story," 51. Candelaria also claimed that the villa occupied four leagues of land. Armijo, "Information Communicated by Juan Candelaria," 275. An undated document directed to Governor Cuervo by the soldiers at Albuquerque declares that the new villa was "certified" on February 23. Cited by Gallagher, "The Founding of Albuquerque," 3.

   Fernando Durán y Chaves and Baltazar Romero, in a petition of 1708, referred to having left their homes at Bernalillo in 1706 and having gone to the new villa of Albuquerque where they were "impelled to take an oath and settle said villa." SANM, I, no. 1205.

23. Armijo, "Information Communicated by Juan Candelaria," 274. Names of the families are provided.

24. All of the preceding testimony, together with a copy of the king's original cédula and a viceregal order, are found in "Testimonio de unas diligencias," Santa Fe, 1712, Misc., SANM, Microfilm Roll 33.

25. *Documentos Para Servir a la Historia del Nuevo México, 1538–1778* (Madrid: Ediciones José Porrúa Turanzas, 1962), 434.

26. Vito Alessio Robles, ed., *Diario y Derrotero de Brigadier Pedro de Rivera* (Mexico: Taller Autográfico, 1946), 51; Hackett, *Historical Documents Relating to New Mexico*, 3: 464; Eleanor B. Adams and Fray Angélico Chávez, eds. and trans., *The Missions of New Mexico, 1776: A Description by Fray Francisco Atanasio Domínguez with other Contemporary Documents* (Albuquerque: University of New Mexico Press, 1956), 151. Spanish law recognized the right of the citizens of a municipality to operate farms and ranches in the adjacent countryside. But it is clear that their main residence was to be in the town and not on such properties. *Recopilación*, book IV, title VIII, law 11.

Chapter Four

1. Petition to the king by Fernando Chacón, 19 November 1802, SANM, II, no. 1629a.

2. Jackson, *The Journals of Zebulon Montgomery Pike*, 1: 415.

3. Herbert E. Bolton, *Coronado, Knight of Pueblo and Plains* (Albuquerque: University of New Mexico Press, 1949), 220–21, 332.

4. Gaspar Pérez de Villagrá, *History of New Mexico* (Los Angeles: Quivira Society, 1933), 179.

5. Hammond and Rey, *Don Juan de Oñate*, 1: 255.

6. Ibid., 104–7, 133.

7. Cited in Eleanor B. Adams and France V. Scholes, "Books in New Mexico, 1598–1680," *NMHR* 17 (July 1942): 269.

8. W. Michael Mathes, "Libros novohispanos de medicina durante el siglo de la Ilustración: 1700–1821," *Colonial Latin American Historical Review* 4 (winter 1995): 55–56. A facsimile edition of the *Suma y Recopilación* was published in Mexico by the Academia Nacional de Medicina, 1977.

9. France V. Scholes and Lansing B. Bloom, "Friar Personnel and Mission Chronology, 1598–1629," *NMHR* 19 (October 1944): 321–23.

10. Gordon Schendel, *Medicine in Mexico* (Austin: University of Texas Press, 1968), 93, 97.

11. A sample inventory of more than 1,100 therapeutic ingredients is, Lista de los remedios y medicinas en la farmacia del Convento Grande, 25 June 1800, Museo Nacional, Mexico, vol. 228. Copy at UNM Spanish Colonial Research Center.

12. Scholes and Bloom, "Friar Personnel," 60, 65. Pedraza had been in New Mexico as early as 1613, so his entry with Eulate in 1618 marked a return.

13. Fray Agustín de Vetancurt, *Teatro Mexicano* (reprint ed., 4 vols.; Madrid: José Porrúa Turanzas, 1960), 4: 270.

14. For the regulatory law on Médicos, Cirujanos, Boticarios, see, *Recopilación de Leyes de los Reynos de las Indias*, lib. v, tit. 6, ley 1.

15. Fernando Ocaranza, *Historia de la medicina en México* (Mexico: Farmacia Midy, 1934), 128. A board of examiners originally named by the cabildo in 1527 had not survived. Schendel, *Medicine in Mexico*, 98–99.

16. Ocaranza, *Historia de la medicina*, 132; and, Manuel Bustos Rodríguez, *Los cirujanos del Real Colegio de Cádiz en la encrucijada de la ilustración, 1748–1796* (Cádiz: Universidad de Cádiz, n.d.), 25–37.

17. For background on the history of pharmacology in New Spain, see Ana María Huerta Jaramillo, *Los boticarios Poblanos: 1536–1825* (Puebla: Gobierno del Estado, 1994), 32–38.

18. Fray Juan Agustín de Morfi, "Geographical Description of New Mexico, 1782," translated in Alfred B. Thomas, *Forgotten Frontiers: A Study of the Spanish Indian Policy of Don Juan Bautista de Anza, Governor of New Mexico, 1777–1787* (Norman: University of Oklahoma Press, 1932), 97.

19. Frederick Webb Hodge, et al., eds., *Fray Alonso de Benavides' Revised Memorial of 1634* (Albuquerque: University of New Mexico Press, 1945), 89.

20. Ibid., 89–90.

21. Fray Agustín de Vetancurt, *Menologio Franciscano* (facsimile ed. of 1697; Mexico: Editorial Porrúa, 1971), 45.

22. Letter of Gov. Fernando de la Concha, 20 November 1788, SANM, II, no. 1023; and Order of Gov. Fernando de la Concha, 15 November 1789, SANM, II, no. 1062.

23. Archives of the Archdiocese of Santa Fe [New Mexico], Loose Documents, Mission, no. 26, 18 August 1815.

24. Warner, "Don Félix Martínez and the Santa Fe Presidio," 270, 304.

25. Fray Angélico Chávez, *Origins of New Mexico Families in the Spanish Colonial Period* (Santa Fe: Historical Society of New Mexico, 1954), 136.

26. George P. Hammond and Agapito Rey, eds. and trans., *The Rediscovery of New Mexico, 1580–1594: The Explorations of Chamuscado, Espejo, Castaño de Sosa, Morlete and Leyva de Bonilla and Humaña* (Albuquerque: University of New Mexico Press, 1966), 111.

27. Hodge, *Fray Alonso de Benavides' Revised Memorial of 1634*, 117.

28. Alfred B. Thomas, trans. and ed., *After Coronado* (Norman: University of Oklahoma Press, 1935), 116. On other surgical procedures resorted to by barbers, see Michael C. Meyer, "Health and Medical Practice on the Northern Frontier of New Spain, 1550–1821," *Locus* 2 (spring 1993): 113.

29. Hackett, *Historical Documents Relating to New Mexico*, 3: 378.

30. Chávez, *Origins of New Mexico Families*, 273; and, Elizabeth Howard West, "The Right of Asylum in New Mexico in the Seventeenth and Eighteenth Centuries," *NMHR* 41 (April 1966): 149–50.

31. The originals of thirty-three Francisco Xavier Romero documents, bound in buffalo hide covers, are owned by a direct descendant, Tomás Romero of La Verne, Calif. who has placed copies in the New Mexico SRCA (Tomás Romero Collection 33J). Mr. Romero has translated and plans to publish these items.

32. Hackett, *Historical Documents Relating to New Mexico*, 3: 401; and Chávez, *Origins of New Mexico Families*, 122.

33. Inventory of the estate of Clemente Gutiérrez, 1785, SANM, I, no. 371; and General Nemesio Salcedo to Governor Real Alencaster, 17 July 1806, SANM, II, no. 2000.

34. Olmsted, *Spanish and Mexican Colonial Censuses of New Mexico*, 8.

35. Christon I. Archer, *The Army in Bourbon Mexico, 1760–1810* (Albuquerque: University of New Mexico Press, 1977), 261–64.

36. Conde de Revilla Gigedo, *Instrucción reservada que dio a su sucesor en el mando, Marqués de Branciforte* (Mexico: Imprenta, a cargo del C. A. Guiol, 1831), art. 684; and, Hospital Militar del Valle de Santa Rosa de Coahuila, 1794–1797, Provincias Internas, vol. 20, leg. 1, Archivo General de la Nación, Mexico.

37. Marc Simmons, *Spanish Government in New Mexico* (Albuquerque: University of New Mexico Press, 1968), 128.

38. See Lansing B. Bloom, *Early Vaccination in New Mexico*, Historical Society of New Mexico Publications, no. 27 (Santa Fe: Santa Fe New Mexican Publishing Corp., 1924; and Michael E. Smith, *The "Real Expedición Marítima de la Vacuna" in New Spain and Guatemala* (Philadelphia: American Philosophical Society, 1974).

39. Pedro Bautista Pino, *The Exposition on the Province of New Mexico, 1812* (Albuquerque: University of New Mexico Press, 1995), 23.

CHAPTER 5

1. The incidence of epidemic disease in other parts of North America has been carefully treated by scholars. Notable works include: John Duffy, *Epidemics in Colonial America* (Baton Rouge: Louisiana State University Press, 1953); and Donald B. Cooper, *Epidemic Disease in Mexico City, 1761–1813* (Austin: Published for the Institute of Latin American Studies by the University of Texas Press, 1965). Concentrating on the Indians are E. Wagner Stearn and Allen E. Stearn, *The Effects of Smallpox on the Destiny of the Amerindian*

(Boston: B. Humphries, Inc., 1945); and P. M. Ashburn, *The Ranks of Death, A Medical History of the Conquest of America* (New York: Coward-McCann, 1947). Both of the Spanish provinces to the east and west of New Mexico have been studied. On Texas see Pat Ireland Nixon, *The Medical Story of Early Texas 1528–1853* (Lancaster, Pa., 1946); and on California consult S. F. Cook, "Smallpox in Spanish and Mexican California, 1770–1845," *Bulletin of the History of Medicine* 7 (1939): 153–91.

2. Benjamin White, *Smallpox and Vaccination* (Cambridge, Mass.: Harvard University Press, 1924), 21.

3. Cooper, *Epidemic Disease in Mexico City*, 63.

4. Duffy, *Epidemics in Colonial America*, 24.

5. Cooper, 65.

6. Sir George Newman, *The Rise of Preventive Medicine* (London: Oxford University Press, H. Milford, 1932), 182–83.

7. Information on vaccination quickly spread throughout the Spanish empire. The story is told by S. F. Cook in "Dr. Francisco Xavier Balmis and the Introduction of Vaccination to Latin America," *Bulletin of the History of Medicine* 11 (1943): 544–55. On the beginning of an immunization program in New Mexico see Lansing B. Bloom, *Early Vaccination in New Mexico.*

8. Declaration of Fray Miguel de Menchero, Santa Bárbara, 10 May 1774, in Hackett, *Historical Documents Relating to New Mexico*, 3: 395–413.

9. Burial Records in Archives of the Archdiocese of Santa Fe (cited hereinafter as AASF), Bur-3, Albuquerque, Box 2. These records have been calendared by Fray Angélico Chávez, *Archives, 1678–1900* (Washington, D.C.: Academy of American Franciscan History, 1957).

10. AASF, Bur-25, San Felipe, Box 13, Chavez, 235, ascribes the statement to Father Irigoyen, but he now tells us that the error resulted from a misreading of his notes.

11. AASF, Bur-49, Santa Fe, Box 27; Bur-51, Santa Fe Castrense, Box 28.

12. SANM, no. 817.

13. Company Roster, SANM, no. 818.

14. Company Roster, 1 April 1781, SANM, no. 820.

15. AASF, Bur-3, Albuquerque, Box 2.

16. Ibid., Bur-46, Sandia, Box 10.

17. Ibid., Bur-25, San Felipe, Box 13.

18. Ibid., Bur-37, Santo Domingo, Box 31.

19. Ibid., Bur-8, Cochiti, Box 6.

20. Ibid., Bur-30, Santa Clara, Box 20.

21. Bancroft, *History of Arizona and New Mexico*, 266.

22. Duffy, 24.

23. Edward B. Vedder, *Medicine, Its Contribution to Civilization* (Baltimore: The Williams & Wilkins Company, 1929), 56.

24. Croix to Anza, Chihuahua, 15 September 1781, SANM, no. 831.

25. Croix to Anza, Chihuahua, 13 January 1783, SANM, no. 850.

26. Cooper, 56.

27. Stearn and Stearn, *Effects of Smallpox*, 40–41.

28. Nixon, *Medical Story of Early Texas*, 46.

29. Herbert E. Bolton, *Athanase de Mézières and the Louisiana-Texas Frontier, 1768–1780,* 2 vols. (Cleveland: The Arthur H. Clark Company, 1914), vol. 1, 27. In the early nineteenth century, Miguel Ramos Arizpe noted that smallpox had devastated the ranks of many fierce nations of western Texas. Benson, *Report of Miguel Ramos Arizpe,* 7.

30. The area west of New Mexico was spared at this time. In 1781 the disease appeared briefly in Lower California, but it was controlled and did not spread to the north. Cook, "Smallpox," 153–55.

31. White, *Smallpox and Vaccination,* 16.

CHAPTER SIX

1. Myrtle Greenfield, *A History of Public Health in New Mexico* (Albuquerque: University of New Mexico Press, 1962).

2. Fernand Braudel, *The Structures of Everyday Life, Civilization and Capitalism* (New York: Harper & Row, 1979), 328.

3. Quoted in J. C. Furnas, *The Americans; A Social History of the United States, 1587–1914* (New York: Putnam, 1969), 140.

4. The problems associated with this venture are described in Terry Lehmann, "Santa Fe and Albuquerque, 1870–1900: Contrast and Conflict in the Development of Two Southwestern Towns" (Ph.D. diss., Indiana University, 1974), 208–10.

5. Marc Simmons, *Albuquerque, A Narrative History* (Albuquerque: University of New Mexico Press, 1982), 228.

6. Tourist and travel writer J. H. Beadle mentions seeing in the 1860s "an occasional square well as large as an ordinary dwelling, cut down into the solid rock, with a never failing supply of water." John Hanson Beadle, *The Undeveloped West, or Five Years in the Territories* (Philadelphia: National Publishing Co., 1873), 504. A reference from the middle eighteenth century suggests the existence of specialized well diggers. "We employed some young men commonly called *balizanes* who as experts in the matter assured us they would obtain water, and having dug until they reached the quicksand, the same thing happened to them as us, and they made their escape and would not dig again even for double the amount." Bernabé Montaño Grant Papers, Records of the Surveyor General, SRCA, roll 34, frame 54.

7. On customs of water transport, see Lewis H. Garrard, *Wah-to-yah and the Taos Trail* (Norman: University of Oklahoma Press, 1955), 180; W. W. Hill, *An Ethnography of Santa Clara Pueblo, New Mexico,* ed. Charles H. Lange (Albuquerque: University of New Mexico Press, 1981), 40–41.

   In 1582 Hernán Gallegos noted that the tinajas of the Pueblo women had pottery lids. He also remarked that "the Indians make and place on their heads a cushion of palm [yucca] leaves, similar to those used in Old Castile, on top of which they place and carry the water jar." Hammond and Rey, *The Rediscovery of New Mexico,* 85. In the nineteenth century, Hispanic women at the village of Tejon, north of the Sandia Mountains, were obliged to transport water on their heads from a spring two and one-half miles away. Lou Sage Batchen, *Las Placitas: Historical Facts and Legends* (Las Placitas, New Mexico: Tumbleweed Press, 1972), 12. For comfort, Pueblo women sometimes used a small cushion or ring of woven yucca leaves on their heads under the tinajas.

8. Thomas B. Hall, M.D., *Medicine on the Santa Fe Trail* (Dayton, Ohio: Morningside Bookshop, 1971), 91. See also Edward W. Moore, "Water," in Milton J. Rosenau, *Preventive Medicine and Public Health*, ed. Kenneth F. Maxey (New York: Appleton-Century-Crofts, 1956), 1133–34. Intestinal parasites, particularly pinworms, may have been endemic among the Hispanic population, as they were among the prehistoric Pueblos. Charles F. Merbs, "Patterns of Health and Sickness in the Precontact Southwest," in David Hurst Thomas, ed., *Columbian Consequences*, 3 vols. (Washington, D.C.: Smithsonian Institution Press, 1989), 1: 46–47.

9. Hill, *Santa Clara Pueblo*, 41. During celebrations attending arrival of the railroad at Albuquerque in 1881, barrels of native wine were placed on the plaza. To each was chained a tin cup from which all passersby were permitted to drink. Communal use of drinking utensils, in this manner, was an old practice. Simmons, *Albuquerque*, 221.

10. Stephen J. Kunitz, M.D., "Disease and Death among the Anasazi, Some Notes on Southwestern Paleoepidemiology," *El Palacio* 76 (June 1976): 19.

11. George Wilkins Kendall, *Narrative of the Texan Santa Fé Expedition*, 2 vols. (Austin, Tex.: The Steck Co., 1935), 1: 277.

12. George Frederick Ruxton, *Ruxton of the Rockies*, ed. LeRoy R. Hafen (Norman: University of Oklahoma Press, 1950), 188.

13. Ibid., 195.

14. Sleeping in the streets of Santa Fe is reported by George Rutledge Gibson, *Journal of a Soldier Under Kearny and Doniphan, 1846–1847* (Glendale, Calif.: Arthur H. Clark Co., 1935), 231. Another soldier observed the same practice at the village of Galisteo. Richard Smith Elliott, *Notes Taken in Sixty Years* (St. Louis, Mo.: R. P. Studley Co., 1883), 242.

15. Susan Shelby Magoffin, *Down the Santa Fe Trail and Into Mexico, the Diary of Susan Shelby Magoffin, 1846–1847*, ed. Stella M. Drumm (New Haven, Conn.: Yale University Press, 1926), 183.

16. Charles W. Gay, Jr. and Don D. Dwyer, *New Mexico Range Plants*, Circular 347, Cooperative Extension Service (Las Cruces: New Mexico State University, 1965): 52.

17. Charles F. Lummis, *A Tramp Across the Continent* (New York: Charles Scribner's Sons, 1892), 187. The handleless "Spanish" broom may in fact have been borrowed from the Pueblo Indians. The style can occasionally be found in use to this day.

18. Gibson, *Journal of a Soldier*, 221. For a brief history of brooms in frontier English America, see Richardson Wright, *Hawkers & Walkers in Early America: Strolling Peddlers, Preachers, Lawyers, Doctors, Players, and Others, from the Beginning to the Civil War* (Philadelphia: J. B. Lippincott, 1927), 63–65.

19. Hog fat apparently was not used for soapmaking in New Mexico until the latter nineteenth century. Sometimes, feral burros were also hunted and killed for their fat. Fabiola Cabeza de Vaca, *We Fed Them Cactus* (Albuquerque: University of New Mexico Press, 1954), 136.

20. For a thorough treatment of potash production in the English colonies, see Robert P. Multhauf, "Potash," in Brooke Hindle, ed., *Material Culture of the Wooden Age* (Tarrytown, N.Y.: Sleepy Hollow Press, 1981), 227–40. General background on the history of soapmaking is given in Norman J. G.

Pounds, *Hearth & Home: A History of Material Culture* (Bloomington: Indiana University Press, 1989), 192–93. The method of soap manufacture in Chihuahua, which was perhaps similar to that prevailing in New Mexico, is described in detail in Eugene H. Boudreau, *Ways of the Sierra Madre* (Sebastopol, Calif.: Pleasant Hills Press, 1974), 51–54.

21. Olibama Lopez Tushar, *The People of "El Valle": A History of the Spanish Colonials in the San Luis Valley* (Denver: Hirsch Graphics, 1975), 44; and John E. Sunder, ed., *Matt Field on the Santa Fe Trail* (Norman: University of Oklahoma Press, 1960), 216.

22. France V. Scholes, "The Supply Service of the New Mexican Missions," 103.

23. Ross Gordon Montgomery, Watson Smith, and John Otis Brew, *Franciscan Awatobi: The Excavation and Conjectural Reconstruction of a 17th Century Spanish Mission Establishment at a Hopi Indian Town in Northeastern Arizona* (Cambridge, Mass.: Peabody Museum, 1949), 212.

24. Peter Boyd-Bowman, "Two Country Stores in XVIIth Century Mexico," *The Americas: The Academy of American Franciscan History* 28 (1972): 247. As of 1803, Governor Fernando de Chacón stated that as far as he knew no one in New Mexico was then "dedicated to the manufacture of soap," and he indicates that soap was being imported from Chihuahua. Marc Simmons, *Coronado's Land: Essays on Daily Life in New Mexico* (Albuquerque: University of New Mexico Press, 1991), 166, 170.

25. Regulations and Accounts of the Santa Fe Presidial Company, Santa Fe, 17 April 1805, SANM.

26. See, for example, Charles Raber, "Personal Recollections of Life on the Plains From 1860 to 1868," *The Westport Historical Quarterly* 7 (December 1971): 8. By the 1870s "Collier's Soap Works" existed six miles east of Fort Union, near the foot of the Turkey Mountains. Nothing is known of its history or operation. *Santa Fe Weekly New Mexican*, 14 January 1871. In 1883 a large soap factory was under construction in Las Cruces and several more were already in operation, manufacturing soap from the amole plant. Peter Hertzog, *The Gringo & Greaser* (Santa Fe: Press of the Territorian, 1964), 10.

27. Padrones de Nuevo México, 1779, Santa Fe, Biblioteca Nacional, Mexico City, legajo 10, numero 59. (From a photocopy in Special Collections, General Library, University of New Mexico, Albuquerque.)

28. Samuel H. Lamb, *Woody Plants of New Mexico*, Bulletin number 14 (Santa Fe: New Mexico Department of Game and Fish, 1971): 46–47.

29. L. S. M. Curtin, *Healing Herbs of the Upper Rio Grande Valley* (Santa Fe: Laboratory of Anthropology, 1947), 46.

30. Susan E. Wallace, *The Land of the Pueblos* (New York: George D. Hurst Publishing, 1888), 67.

31. Cleofas M. Jaramillo, *Shadows of the Past* (Santa Fe: Ancient City Press, n.d.), 48.

32. Daniel Ellis Conner, *Joseph Reddeford Walker and the Arizona Adventure* (Norman: University of Oklahoma Press, 1956), 16. A plan of the Santa Fe presidio, 1791, shows two laundries (*lavaderos*) situated over the main water ditch crossing the interior yard. Marc Simmons, *Spanish Government in New Mexico*, xviii.

33. Scholes, "The Supply Service of the New Mexico Missions," 101.

Seventeenth-century friars were each furnished one large brass basin, one razor, and one pair of barber's scissors. Traditionally, corncobs were used as scrubbers to clean dirty knees and elbows of children. Interview with Concha Ortiz y Pino de Kleven, Villanueva, New Mexico, 12 August 1974.

34. W. W. H. Davis, *El Gringo, Or New Mexico & Her People* (Santa Fe: Rydal Press, 1938), 207–8.

35. Susan Magoffin in 1846 mentions another instance of native bathing. At El Paso she recorded that an Indian woman gave birth and a half hour afterward went to the Rio Grande to bathe herself and child, a practice she continued on successive days. Magoffin, *Down the Santa Fe Trail*, 68. In 1841, the priest at El Paso provided Kendall a bath in his private study. Kendall, *The Texan Santa Fé Expedition*, 2: 36.

36. Hans Zinsser, *Rats, Lice and History: Being a Study in Biography, Which after Twelve Preliminary Chapters Indispensable for the Preparation of the Lay Reader, Deals with the Life History of Typhus Fever* (Boston: Atlantic Monthly Press, 1944), 89–90.

37. Hammond and Rey, *Don Juan de Oñate*, 656.

38. Adams, *Bishop Tamarón's Visitation*, 55.

39. Kendall, *The Texan Santa Fé Expedition*, 1: 316, 327.

40. Ibid., 2: 36. The situation Kendall described persisted in some Mexican areas to the mid-twentieth century. See Nathan L. Whetten, *Rural Mexico* (Chicago: University of Chicago Press, 1948), 296.

41. Frank S. Edwards, *A Campaign in New Mexico with Colonel Doniphan* (Philadelphia: Carey and Hart, 1847), 51.

42. Lansing B. Bloom, ed., "Bourke on the Southwest," *NMHR* 11 (July 1936): 260.

43. S. L. Bensusan, *Home Life in Spain* (New York: Macmillan Co., 1910), 11.

44. Wesley Robert Hurt, Jr., "Manzano: A Study of Community Disorganization" (master's thesis, University of New Mexico, 1941), 123.

45. Everett Dick, *Vanguards of the Frontier: A Social History of the Northern Plains and Rocky Mountains from the Earliest White Contacts to the coming of the Homemaker* (Lincoln: University of Nebraska Press, 1965), 320. Marian Sloan Russell wrote that in Santa Fe during the early 1850s her mother periodically carried the family bedsteads outside and poured boiling water on them to get rid of bugs. "She would dip a hen feather in kerosene and oil the places not touched by water." This was probably not a local Hispanic practice but one brought from the East. Mrs. Hal Russell, ed., *Land of Enchantment: Memoirs of Marian Russell on the Santa Fe Trail* (Albuquerque: University of New Mexico Press, 1984), 55.

46. Naomi Zunker Phoenix, "Reminiscences of a Confederate Soldier Who Fought in the Battles of Valverde and Glorieta" (paper presented at the Historical Society of New Mexico Annual Conference, Santa Fe, 27 April 1990).

47. Edwards, *A Campaign in New Mexico*, 51.

48. Elliott, *Notes Taken in Sixty Years*, 242.

49. Reyes N. Martínez, "Delousing," Typescript number 370, WPA manuscripts, History Library, Museum of New Mexico, Santa Fe.

50. Davis, *El Gringo*, 195.

51. Russell, *Land of Enchantment*, 55; and Kenneth Fordyce, "New Mexico Flies," Typescript number 309, WPA manuscripts, History Library, Museum of New Mexico, Santa Fe.

52. Braudel, *The Structures of Everyday Life*, 310.

53. Pounds, *Hearth & Home*, 247.

54. John A. Crow, *Spain: The Root and the Flower: A History of the Civilization of Spain and the Spanish People* (New York: Harper & Row, 1963), 127.

55. Frederick W. Hodge, ed., *Spanish Explorers in the Southern United States, 1528–1543* (New York: Barnes and Noble, 1946), 354.

56. Charles H. Lange and Carroll L. Riley, *The Southwestern Journals of Adolph F. Bandelier,* (Albuquerque: University of New Mexico Press, 1966), vol. 1, 104. In 1881 Lieutenant John G. Bourke, upon spending a night in Jemez Pueblo, complained: "I had no rest last night, my sleep being constantly broken by the movements in and out of the house of men, women, and children answering the calls of nature, there being no household accommodations [sic] for such purposes in Jemez." Bloom, "Bourke on the Southwest," 231.

57. Leslie A. White, *The Pueblo of Sia, New Mexico*, Smithsonian Institution Bureau of American Ethnology, Bulletin 184 (Washington, D.C.: Government Printing Office, 1962), 104.

58. Hackett, *Historical Documents Relating to New Mexico*, 3: 141. This source also notes that in the neighboring pueblo of Las Humanas (Gran Quivira) the residents, owing to a lack of water, saved their urine to mix adobe mud for house building (p. 142). Urine was also used among colonial New Mexicans as a mordant in dying yarn. Roland F. Dickey, *New Mexico Village Arts* (Albuquerque: University of New Mexico Press, 1949), 118. Formerly, the Hispanic housewife would sometimes empty urine from the chamber pots in a circle around the house, believing that it kept stray dogs and snakes away. Interview with Trinidad R. Padilla, Jarales, New Mexico, 1 July 1987.

59. John L. Kessell, *The Missions of New Mexico since 1776* (Albuquerque: University of New Mexico Press, 1980), 97, 201.

60. In the early twentieth century, the Ortiz y Pino family of Galisteo (Santa Fe County) deposited wood ashes in the outdoor latrines. But whether this represented an old or a recently introduced practice is uncertain. Interview with Concha Ortiz y Pino de Kleven, Albuquerque, 2 March 1990.

61. Anthropologist Leslie White declares that at Zia Pueblo in 1957, after privies had been built on the village periphery, many Indians considered them so distant that they tended to use nearby streets and alleys at night. And he adds: "Corrals still serve as latrines." White, *The Pueblo of Sia, New Mexico*, 104. At colonial Williamsburg, scavenger chickens cleaned up human waste. Personal communication, Doss Brown to Marc Simmons, Philadelphia, 17 February 1982. During the 1840s, roaming herds of pigs in New York City and Cincinnati ate ordure and garbage that filled the streets. Furnas, *The Americans; A Social History*, 455–56.

   At Bent's Fort on the Arkansas River in 1847, young Lewis H. Garrard observed a dog of "the Mexican shepherd breed" that prowled about "on watch for offal and other refuse." Garrard, *Wah-to-yah and the Taos Trail*, 131. James F. Downs, conducting fieldwork among the Navajos in 1960 and 1961, wrote that dogs played an important role because of the informal toilet arrangements of the average Navajo home. He states: "Small children relieve their bowels wherever they happen to be. The evidence, however, quickly disappears because a defecating child is immediately circled by several none-too-patient canines. Adults who withdraw from camp to defecate are usually followed by dogs. Dogs also consume fresh horse and cow dung, . . . thus keeping the home site relatively free of filth and flies." James F. Downs, *The Navajo* (New York: Holt, Rinehart and Winston, 1972), 53. Such a situation once may have been fairly general among New Mexican populations.

62. A copper chamber pot was included in a 1755 inventory of San José Mission, Texas. Fr. Marion A. Habig, comp., *The San José Papers* (San Antonio, Tex.: Old Spanish Missions Historical Research Library, 1978), 14. The estate of a soldier who died in Nueva Vizcaya in 1642 included "a little silver chamber pot." Peter Boyd-Bowman, "A Spanish Soldier's Estate in Northern Mexico," *Hispanic American Historical Review* 53 (February 1973): 102.

63. Florence C. Lister and Robert H. Lister, "One Pot's Pedigree," in Nancy L. Fox, ed., *Collected Papers in Honor of Charlie R. Steen, Jr.* (Albuquerque: Albuquerque Archaeological Society Press, 1983), 167–87; and, Patricia R. Vickman, "Spanish Chamber Pots," *St. Augustine Archaeological Association* (St. Augustine, Fla.: St. Augustine Archaeological Association, 1989), 2–3.

64. An apparent example of an Indian-made chamber pot, dating from the colonial era, was on display recently at Quarai Mission, Salinas National Monument, New Mexico. It is a fired red ware, undecorated and lacking handles, cylindrical in shape, with a flared rim.

65. As early as the year 1388, the English parliament passed the first nationwide antipollution act to clean up the air and waters. Spain's interest in the issue did not surface until the early modern period. Jean Gimpel, *The Medieval Machine: The Industrial Revolution of the Middle Ages* (New York: Holt, Rinehart and Winston, 1976), 87.

66. *Recopilación de Leyes de los Reynos de las Indias,* libro IV, titulo 7; and Dan Stanislawski, "Early Spanish Town Planning in the New World," *Geographical Review* 35 (January 1947): 102.

67. For a discussion of public health administration in New Spain's capital, see Donald B. Cooper, *Epidemic Disease in Mexico City, 1761–1813: An Administrative, Social, and Medical Study* (Austin: University of Texas Press, 1965), 16–46.

68. Journal of the Municipal Corporation of Santa Fe, 1824–1834 (translation in typescript by George P. Hammond), doc. P-E 233, Bancroft Library, Berkeley, California.

69. Marc Simmons, ed. and trans., "Antonio Barreiro's 1833 Proclamation on Santa Fe City Government," *El Palacio* 76 (June 1970): 24–30.

70. The ordinances were first published in the [Albuquerque] *Rio Abajo Weekly Press,* May 5 and 12, 1863. They were reprinted as *Town Ordinances of Albuquerque, New Mexico, 1863* (Albuquerque: Vinegar Tom Press, 1970).

71. *Rio Abajo Weekly Press,* 14 April 1863.

CHAPTER 7

1. Luís Navarro García, *Sonora y Sinaloa en el siglo XVII* (Sevilla: Escuela de Estudios Hispano-Americanos, 1967), 67–68; Chávez, *Origins of New Mexico Families*, 88–89; Robert C. West, *The Mining Community in Northern New Spain: The Parral Mining District* (Berkeley: University of California Press, 1949), 6–12, 81–88, 90.

2. Moorhead, *New Mexico's Royal Road*, 28–54.

3. Of this recruitment, contemporary Spanish historian Luís Navarro García has remarked with some wonder: "who could imagine that New Mexico, so early, would become a mother-agent in helping to populate other provinces. Reasonably one might think of Tlaxcala or Zacatecas in these terms, but never Santa Fe. Yet here is a curious incident, now forgotten, linking the first Sonorans with the people of New Mexico." Navarro García, *Sonora y Sinaloa*, 68. Pedro Perea also enlisted five New Mexican Franciscans to work in Sonora. Their ensuing conflict with the Jesuits of that province is discussed in Charles W. Polzer, S.J., ed., "The Franciscan Entrada into Sonora, 1645–1652: A Jesuit Chronicle," *Arizona and the West* XIV (autumn 1972): 253–78. Polzer also refers to trips to Sonora in the 1630s by Governor Luis de Rosas and Fray Tomás Manso of New Mexico. For additional details, see Albert H. Schroeder, ed., "Southwestern Chronicle: The Cipias and Ypotlapiguas," *Arizona Quarterly* XII (summer 1956): 101–9; and Chávez, *Origins of New Mexico Families*, 88–89.

4. Francisco R. Almada, *Diccionario de Historia, Geografía y Biografía Sonorenses* (Chihuahua: Ruiz Sandoval, 1952), 722; Scholes, *Troublous Times in New Mexico*, 44–45, 52, 123; Hackett, *Historical Documents Relating to New Mexico*, 3: 261–62.

5. Hackett, *Historical Documents Relating to New Mexico*, 3: 269, 271.

6. Ibid., 3: 271–77.

7. Herbert E. Bolton, trans. & ed., *Kino's Historical Memoir of Pimería Alta*, 2 vols. (Cleveland: Arthur H. Clark Company, 1919), I, 53n; Manuel Espinosa, *Crusaders of the Rio Grande* (Chicago: Institute of Jesuit History, 1942), 44.

8. Bolton, *Kino's Historical Memoir*, I, 53n; Espinosa, *Crusaders of the Rio Grande*, 39–40; Jack D. Forbes, *Apache, Navaho, and Spaniard* (Norman: University of Oklahoma Press, 1960), 230.

9. Espinosa, *Crusaders of the Rio Grande*, 336n.

10. Bancroft, *History of Arizona and New Mexico*, 365.

11. An account of the Menchero expedition of 1747 is in John L. Kessell, "Campaigning on the Upper Gila, 1756," *NMHR* 46 (April 1971): 135–39. According to the author, the Spaniards prepared a map and kept journals of the expedition, but these have not been found. Report of Alonso Victores Rubí de Celís of an Expedition Against the Gila Apaches, 6–26 December 1747, document 483, Spanish Archives of New Mexico, State Records Center [SRC], Santa Fe.

12. Father Bartolomé Saenz's report on the Bustamante-Vildósola expedition is published in Kessell, "Campaigning on the Upper Gila," *NMHR* 46: 145–51. For the services by Opatá auxiliaries on the southwestern frontier, see Oakah L. Jones, *Pueblo Warriors and Spanish Conquest* (Norman: University of Oklahoma Press, 1966), 24–29. A document illustrating the

use of Sonoran Opatás in southern New Mexico is Muster of Troops participating in Navajo Campaign, Arizpe, 22 October 1804, doc. 1768, SANM, SRC.

13. Charles E. Chapman, *The Founding of Spanish California* (New York: Macmillan, 1916), 44. Fray Francisco Garcés to the minister of Zuni, Moqui, 3 July 1776, in Adams and Chávez, *The Missions of New Mexico, 1776,* 283. Examples of the many records concerning Garcés are in expedients 10 and 17, volume 52, Historia, Archivo General de la Nación [AGN], Mexico City. E. M. Coues, ed., *On the Trail of a Spanish Pioneer: The Diary and Itinerary of Francisco Garcés,* 2 vols. (New York: F. P. Harper, 1900).

14. Ynforme del Gobernador Don Pedro Fermín de Mendinueta sobre comunicación con Sonora, Santa Fe, 9 November 1775, exp. 13, vol. 52, Historia, AGN.

15. Mario Hernández Sánchez-Barba, *Juan Bautista de Anza, Un Hombre de Fronteras* (Madrid: Publicaciones Españoles, 1962), 115–16.

16. Pedro Vial, a Frenchman in the employ of Spain, blazed trails from Santa Fe east to San Antonio, Natchitoches, and St. Louis between 1786 and 1806, but a lack of resources prevented a follow up of his discoveries. The most recent work on Vial is Noel M. Loomis & Abraham P. Nasatir, *Pedro Vial and the Roads to Santa Fe* (Norman: University of Oklahoma Press, 1967). Included is a translation of the 1808 diary of Francisco Amangual, describing another attempt to open a road between Santa Fe and San Antonio. Father Silvestre Vélez de Escalante, looking in the other direction, hoped to open a route from Santa Fe, west to Monterrey in California. As missionary at Zuni he had probed westward in the early 1770s only to find the way blocked by hostile Apaches. Therefore, in 1776 he set out with Father Atanasio Domínguez on a more roundabout trail that led from Santa Fe northwestward through the Great Basin toward the California settlements. Severe winter weather in western Utah, however, forced the party to turn back to New Mexico. Herbert E. Bolton, *Pageant in the Wilderness: The Story of the Escalante Expedition to the Interior Basin, 1776* (new ed., Salt Lake City: Utah State Historical Society, 1972).

17. Anza's view on trade is in Pedro Galindo Navarro to Teodoro de Croix, 28 July 1789, quoted in Thomas, *Forgotten Frontiers,* 180. A condemnation of the Chihuahua trade monopoly is in Fray Agustín de Morfí, Desordenes que se advierten en el Nuevo México, 1778, vol. 25, Historia, AGN; Fernando Ocaranza, *Crónicas y relaciones del occidente de México,* 2 vols. (Mexico: n. p., 1939), II, 203. On Sonoran mining and labor problems during this period, see Sanford A. Mosk, "Economic Problems in Sonora in the Late Eighteenth Century," *Pacific Historical Review* VIII (September 1939): 341–45.

18. Mapa de Rocha, 1784, reproduced in Luís Navarro García, *José de Gálvez y la comandancia general de las Provincias Internas* (Sevilla: Escuela de Estudios Hispano-Americanos, 1964), plate 113. See also Vito Alessio Robles, ed., *Nicolás de LaFora, Relación del viaje que hizo a los presidios internos* (Mexico: Editorial Pedro Robredo, 1939), 119.

19. Dictamen del Ingeniero D. Miguel Constansó sobre distancias del Nuevo México a Sonora y a Monterrey, México, 18 March 1776, exp. 2, vol. 169, Provincias Internas, AGN.

20. The Hopi expedition is in Thomas, *Forgotten Frontiers*, 19–30, 38, 227–39. Anza's diary was first translated by Ralph E. Twitchell, and published as *Colonel Juan Bautista de Anza, Governor of New Mexico, Diary of His Expedition to the Moquis in 1780* (Santa Fe: Historical Society of New Mexico, 1918).

21. Adams, *Bishop Tamarón's Visitation*, 39.

22. Thomas, *Forgotten Frontiers*, 35. El Cavallero de Croix to Juan Bautista de Anza, Arizpe, 30 December 1779, doc. 777, SANM, SRC.

23. Extracto de Revista, Santa Fe Presidial Company, 1 February 1781, doc. 817, SANM, SRC; Navarro García, *José de Gálvez*, 385–86. Anza asked Croix to have the Sonoran and Nueva Vizcayan companies meet him on the Río San Francisco in mid November. If he failed to join them at the appointed time, they should return to their bases, understanding that he had found a more favorable route in another direction. Thomas, *Forgotten Frontiers*, 37–38. The Fray Cristóbal camp site, located on the Camino Real at the north end of the Jornada del Muerto, was named for Fray Juan Cristóbal, one of the friars accompanying Oñate in 1598.

24. Alfred B. Thomas, *Teodoro de Croix and the Northern Frontier of New Spain, 1776–1783* (Norman: University of Oklahoma Press, 1941), 110–11. Anza's diary of his Sonora trip is translated in Thomas, *Forgotten Frontiers*, 195–205. A copy of the original diary is in Diario de derroteros apostólicos y militares, vol. 24, Historia, AGN.

25. Anza died at Arizpe on 19 December 1778, and was buried in the church of Nuestra Señora de la Asunción. A description of the Echeagaray expedition is in the introductory notes to George P. Hammond, "The Zuniga Journal, Tucson to Santa Fé: The opening of a Spanish Trade Route, 1788–1795," *NMHR* 6 (January 1931): 41–48. Hammond stated that he had not been able to locate the Echeagaray journal. This document is in Diario de la campaña executada por el Capitán don Manuel de Echeagaray contra los Apaches de los Mimbres y otros Gileños Orientales, Año de 1788, exp. 4, vol. 128, Provincias Internas, AGN.

26. Concha's expedition is in Concha to Nava, El Paso, 24 January 1792, doc. 1187, SANM, SRC. Concha mentions that he kept a diary of his campaign, but this has not come to light.

27. Ibid. Pedro de Nava to the Conde de Revilla Gigedo, Chihuahua, 20 January 1792, vol. 62, Provincias Internas, AGN; Thomas, *Forgotten Frontiers*, 40.

28. Proclamation of Manuel Echeagaray, Arizpe, 31 March 1795, doc. 1322, SANM, SRC. Circa 1793 Capitan Don Pedro de Allende led a Spanish column from Terrenate via Tucson to the Gila to scout for Apaches. Carl Sauer, "A Spanish Expedition into the Arizona Apachería," *Arizona Historical Review* VI (January 1935): 3–13. Sauer includes a map. Echeagaray commanded one of the detachments.

29. Zúñiga letter, dated at Zuni, 1 May 1795, is doc. 1321, SANM, SRC. See also, Hammond, "Zúñiga Journal," *NMHR* 6: 40–65.

30. Hammond, "Zúñiga Journal," *NMHR* 6: 52.

31. Joseph Miguel de la Peña and Vicente Sena to Pedro Fermín de Mendinueta, Arizpe, 21 June 1780, number 60, legajo 10, Biblioteca Nacional de México, Mexico City; Thomas, *Forgotten Frontiers*, 177–78.

32. Documents 1159, 1563, 1688, 1715, SANM, SRC; Governor of New

Mexico to Nemesio Salcedo, Santa Fe, 19 November 1809, doc. 2269, ibid. The list of goods mentioned by the governor has disappeared from the archives.

33. Lange and Riley, *The Southwestern Journals of Adolph F. Bandelier*, vol. 2, 237.

CHAPTER 8

1. Hammond and Rey, *Don Juan de Oñate*, 2: 665.

2. Odie B. Faulk, "Ranching in Spanish Texas," *Hispanic American Historical Review* 45 (May 1965): 257.

3. Alicia Ronstadt Milich, ed. and trans., *Relaciones of Zarate Salmerón* (Albuquerque: Horn and Wallace, 1966), 55.

4. Charles Wilson Hackett and Charmion C. Shelby, *Historical Documents Relating to New Mexico, Nueva Vizcaya, and Approaches Thereto, to 1773*, 3 vols. (Washington, D.C.: Carnegie Institution, 1923–1937), 3: 71.

5. Lynn I. Perrigo, ed. and trans., "Provincial Statutes of 1824 to 1826," *NMHR* 27 (January 1952): 66.

6. Padrones de Nuevo México, 1779, Biblioteca Nacional, leg. 10, doc. 59, Archivo General de la Nación, Mexico.

7. SANM, II, no. 1164 (3), State Records Center and Archives, Santa Fe.

8. Benjamin M. Read, *Illustrated History of New Mexico* (Santa Fe: New Mexican Printing Co., 1912), 505.

9. Faulk, "Ranching in Spanish Texas," 266; and Sandra L. Myers, "The Ranching Frontier," in Harold M. Hollingsworth and Sandra L. Myers, eds., *Essays on the American West* (Austin: University of Texas Press, 1969), 21.

10. Terry G. Jordan, *Trails to Texas* (Lincoln: University of Nebraska Press, 1981), 17.

11. Josiah Gregg, *Commerce of the Prairies,* ed. Max L. Moorhead (reprint ed., Norman: University of Oklahoma Press, 1954), 131.

12. Garrard, *Wah-to-yah and the Taos Trail*, 144–47.

13. John E. Rouse, *The Criollo: Spanish Cattle in the Americas* (Norman: University of Oklahoma Press, 1977), 238.

14. John C. Ewers, "Spanish Cattle in Plains Indian Art," *Great Plains Journal* 16 (fall 1976): 68.

15. Hammond and Rey, *Don Juan de Oñate*, 1: 145.

16. Rouse, *The Criollo*, 224–25.

17. Thomas, *Forgotten Frontiers*, 108.

CHAPTER 9

1. On the looseness of Spanish law regarding the matter of irrigation, Marcelino C. Peñuelas says, "En las *Leyes de Indias* se establecen normas concretas sobre trabajos de irrigación pública. Sin embargo, estas normas eran lo suficientemente amplias para permitir adaptaciones a las especiales condiciones de cada región." *Lo Español en el Suroeste de los Estados Unidos* (Madrid: Ediciones Cultura Hispánica, 1964), 272–75.

2. Éléna de la Souchère, *An Explanation of Spain* (New York: Random House, 1965), 16.

3. See for example, George M. Foster, *Culture and Conquest, America's Spanish Heritage* (reprint ed., Chicago: Quadrangle Books, 1960), 62; and John G. Bourke, "Notes on the Language and Folk-usage of the Rio Grande Valley, With Special Regard to the Survivals of Arabic Custom," *Journal of American Folklore* 9 (1896): 115.

4. West, *The Mining Community in Northern New Spain*, 70.

5. Louis Bertrand and Charles Petrie, *The History of Spain* (2nd ed., London, 1952), 34, 138, 253–54.

6. W. Montgomery Watt, *A History of Islamic Spain* (Garden City, N.Y., 1967), 40.

7. Gordon R. Willey, *An Introduction to American Archeology*, 2 vols. (Englewood Cliffs, N.J., 1962), 1: 213. See also F. W. Hodge, "Prehistoric Irrigation in Arizona," *American Anthropologist* 6 (1893): 323–30.

8. Herbert W. Yeo, "An Old Ditch," *New Mexico Highway Journal* 7 (1929): 23.

9. Lange and Riley, *The Southwestern Journals of Adolph F. Bandelier*, 1: 79.

10. Willey, *American Archeology*, 1: 213.

11. Hammond and Rey, *The Rediscovery of New Mexico*, 182, 224.

12. Albert H. Schroeder and Dan S. Matson, eds. & trans., *A Colony on the Move, Gaspar Castaño de Sosa's Journal, 1590–1591* (Santa Fe: School of American Research, 1965), 118.

13. Adolph F. Bandelier, *Final Report of Investigations Among the Indians of the Southwestern United States* (Cambridge, Mass.: J. Wilson and son, 1890), 237.

14. George F. Carter, *Plant Geography and Culture History in the American Southwest* (New York, 1944), 114.

15. Joe Ben Wheat, "Kroeber's Formulation of the Southwestern Culture Area," *University of Colorado Studies*, Series in Anthropology, no. 4 (Boulder: University of Colorado Press, 1954), 32.

16. Edward P. Dozier, "The Pueblos of the Southwestern United States," *Journal of the Royal Archeological Institute* 90 (1960): 150.

17. Hammond and Rey, *Don Juan de Oñate*, 2: 610, 626.

18. Pérez de Villagrá, *History of New Mexico*, 148.

19. The Ordinances of 1573 are printed in *Colección de Documentos Inéditos Relativos al Descubrimiento, Conquista y Organización de las Antiguas Posesiones Españolas de América y Oceanía*, 42 vols. (Madrid, 1864–1884), 16: 154.

20. Ireneo L. Chaves, trans., "Instructions to Peralta by Viceroy," *NMHR* 4 (July 1929): 181. In some instances on the northern frontier of New Spain, the governor, usually in absence of a cabildo, was delegated the power to allot land and water rights to new citizens. Such a case occurred in 1730 in the province of Texas. Spell, "The Grant and First Survey of the City of San Antonio," 76.

21. Reference to an acequia madre on the north side of the river is found in a document cited by Ralph E Twitchell, *Old Santa Fe* (Chicago: Rio Grande Press, 1963), 78–79. This canal became known as the Acequia de la Muralla because of its proximity to a wall defending the northern limits of the town. Ibid., 56.

22. Adams, *Bishop Tamarón's Visitation*, 35.

23. Lansing B. Bloom, ed. & trans., "Albuquerque and Galisteo, Certificate of the Founding, 1706," *NMHR* 10 (January 1935): 48.

24. Adams and Chávez, *The Missions of New Mexico, 1776*, 151.

25. Twitchell, *Spanish Colonization in New Mexico*, 20.

26. *Recopilación de Leyes de los Reynos de las Indias*, lib. iv, tit. xvii, leyes 5–14.

27. Joaquín Escriche y Martín, *Diccionario Razonado de Legislación y Jurisprudencia* (new ed., Paris: Rosa, Bouret y Cia, 1852), 64–65.

28. Wells A. Hutchins, "The Community Acequia: Its Origin and Development," *Southwestern Historical Quarterly* 31 (1927–28): 267.

29. Peñuelas, *Lo Español*, 272–74; and, Foster, *Culture and Conquest*, 64.

30. Hutchins, "The Community Acequia," 271.

31. Fernando Chacón to Jacobo Ugarte, Santa Fe, 14 June 1802, SANM, no. 1607.

32. John Preston Moore, *The Cabildo in Peru Under the Hapsburgs* (Durham, N.C.: Duke University Press, 1954), 70.

33. That Santa Fe now has a mayordomo (as of 1971, Ignacio Moya) over its acequia madre, is no evidence that this official existed under Spanish rule, although such may have been the case.

34. Josiah Gregg refers to supervision of ditch work by alcaldes during the Mexican period. *Commerce of the Prairies*, 108. Regulations governing irrigation matters and composed by Alcalde Mayor Ignacio Sánchez Vergara may be found in Marc Simmons, ed. & trans., "An Alcalde's Proclamation, A Rare New Mexico Document," *El Palacio* 75 (1968): 8–9.

35. Davis, *El Gringo*, 69; and, William Blackmore, *The Spanish-Mexican Land Grants of New Mexico and Colorado, 1863–1878*, 2 vols. (Denver, 1949), 1: 12.

36. Lista de los Dueños de Terreno Bajo el Regadio de la Acequia Nueva del Chamisal y Sus Medidos, ca. 1845, Misc. Papers, Archives of the Archdiocese of Santa Fe. Of related interest from the twentieth century is "Rules of a Community Ditch System," *NMHR* 34 (1959): 307.

37. Davis, *El Gringo*, 70–71.

38. Frances Leon Swadesh, *Hispanic Americans of the Ute Frontier from the Chama Valley to the San Juan Basin, 1694–1960*, Report no. 50 (Boulder: University of Colorado, Tri-ethnic Research Project, 1966), 163.

39. Gregg, *Commerce of the Prairies*, 108.

40. Another device, the ancient water lift or noria which supplied acequias from a well, was used in some of the north Mexican provinces but apparently never reached the Southwest.

41. Hackett, *Historical Documents Relating to New Mexico*, 3: 507.

42. James William Abert, *Abert's New Mexico Report, 1846–'47* (Albuquerque: Horn & Wallace, 1962), 107.

43. Instances of such dam destruction as recently as the 1930s on the Puerco and Pecos Rivers are described in Jerold Gwayn Widdison, "Historical Geography of the Middle Rio Puerco Valley, New Mexico," *NMHR* 34: 276; and Olen E. Leonard, *The Role of the Land Grant in the Social Organization and Social Processes of a Spanish-American Village in New Mexico* (Albuquerque: Calvin Horn Publications, 1970), 64.

44. Hutchins, "The Community Acequia," 274.

45. Davis, *El Gringo*, 67.

46. Twitchell, *Old Santa Fe*, 79n; and, Adams and Chávez, *The Missions of New Mexico, 1776*, 71n.

47. Gregg, *Commerce of the Prairies*, 108.

48. Farmers, following traditional practices today, are often observed over-watering their fields on the theory that if some moisture is good for the crops, more must be better. The result is a rapid leaching of minerals from the soil and a significant reduction of food value in the crops produced. This may have been a problem also in the colonial period during years when water was abundant. Interview with David Carter, Soil Conservation Officer, Pecos, N.M., 20 February 1971.

49. See Governor Real Alencaster to Commandant General Salcedo, Santa Fe, 1 September 1806, SANM, no. 2012(3), in which the governor refers to the misery and famine caused by a general lack of water for planting.

50. Simmons, "An Alcalde's Proclamation," 9. In the context of this document the term *canoa* clearly means flume. More often in New Mexico it meant a hollowed out log that served as a water trough or salt box for livestock. During the Mexican period, alcaldes in Santa Fe were obliged to see that irrigation ditches crossing roads were provided with bridges and that all acequias were so placed as to avoid flooding of the streets. Marc Simmons, trans., "Antonio Barreiro's 1833 Proclamation on Santa Fe City Government," *El Palacio* 76 (June 1970): 29.

51. *Recopilación*, Lib. ii, tit. I, ley 4; and, Hutchins, "The Community Acequia," 266.

52. In an interesting case from the early Mexican period, the alcalde of Bernalillo, upon complaint of Santa Ana Indians, required a local settler to contribute his share of labor to a common acequia. Testimony taken by Jesús Miera, Bernalillo, 18 July 1829, Julius Seligman Collection, University of New Mexico Library, Albuquerque.

53. Hackett, *Historical Documents Relating to New Mexico*, 3: 507.

54. Lansing B. Bloom, ed., "A Glimpse of New Mexico in 1620," *NMHR* 3 (1928): 369.

55. Bando of Pedro Reneros de Posada, El Paso del Norte, 3 March 1687, SANM, no. 43.

56. Bando of Pedro de Villasur, Santa Fe, 11 August 1718, SANM, no. 290.

57. Simmons, "An Alcalde's Proclamation," 8. The problem of errant livestock continued well into the twentieth century. An act of the Fourth New Mexico State Legislature, *Leyes de Nuevo México*, 1919, 191–97, concerning damage to irrigation ditches by stray stock was, in tone, strongly reminiscent of the Jemez alcalde's proclamation on the same matter.

CHAPTER 10

1. John Francis McDermott, ed., *Travels in Search of the Elephant: The Wanderings of Alfred S. Waugh, Artist, in Louisiana, Missouri, and Santa Fe, in 1845–1846* (St. Louis: Missouri Historical Society, 1951), 125.

2. Gerald Brenan, *South From Granada* (Baltimore: Penguin Books, 1963), 127.

3. Charles F. Lummis, *Mesa, Cañon and Pueblo* (New York: Century Co., 1925), 207.

4. Gregg, *Commerce of the Prairies*, 169–70; and Davis, *El Gringo*, 60–61.

5. WPA typescript, "Life in the Old Houses," #61, New Mexico State Library, Santa Fe.

6. Sir James George Frazer, *The Golden Bough, A Study in Magic and Religion* (New York: MacMillan Co., 1960), 80, 177–78, 750.

7. Thomas J. Steele, S.J., *Santos and Saints* (Albuquerque: Calvin Horn Publications, 1974), 187.

8. Brenan, *South From Granada,* 127; and, Foster, *Culture and Conquest,* 75.

9. Brenan, 129; and, Foster, 198.

10. Brenan, 128–29.

11. Foster, 199.

12. Antonio Arribas, *The Iberians* (New York: Frederick A. Praeger, 1964), 131; and, Edwyn Hole, *Andalus: Spain Under the Moslems* (London: Robert Hole, Ltd., 1958), 27.

13. Alex Dundes, *The Cockfight* (Madison: University of Wisconsin Press, 1994), vii; and, George F. Carter, "Pre-Columbian Chickens in America," in Carroll L. Riley, et al., *Man Across the Sea, Problems of Pre-Columbian Contacts* (Austin: University of Texas Press, 1971), 212.

14. Foster, 176–77.

15. Marcelin Defourneaux, *Daily Life in Spain in the Golden Age* (New York: Praeger Publications, 1971), 133; Luis Weckmann, *The Medieval Heritage of Mexico* (New York: Fordham University Press, 1992), 408; and, R. Trevor Davies, *The Golden Century of Spain, 1501–1621* (New York: Harper and Row, 1961), 132–33.

16. Pérez de Villagrá, *History of New Mexico*, 141.

17. Gregg, *Commerce of the Prairies,* 169–70.

18. Lorin W. Brown, *Hispano Folklife of New Mexico* (Albuquerque: University of New Mexico Press, 1978), 175.

19. *Among the Pueblo Indians* (New York: Merriam Co., 1895), 63.

20. "San Juan's Day at Cochiti Pueblo, New Mexico, 1894 and 1947," *El Palacio* 59 (June 1952): 178.

21. Kate L. Gregg, ed., *The Road to Santa Fe, The Journal and Diaries of George Champlin Sibley* (reprint ed., Albuquerque: University of New Mexico Press, 1995), 135.

22. Foster states that to commemorate San Juan fires were commonly lighted in Spanish America. He also suggests that while America's San Juan observances were similar to those of Spain, they were perhaps less intense. *Culture and Conquest*, 208, n. 6.

23. Aurelio M. Espinosa, "New Mexican Spanish Folklore," *The Journal of American Folklore* 23 (Oct.–Dec. 1910): 416. In many communities, Vespers (evening prayers) was a fixture of St. John's Eve.

24. Cleofas M. Jaramillo, *Shadows of the Past*, 85.

25. Interview with Concha Ortiz y Pino de Kleven, Santa Fe, 29 August 1999. Within a decade, most of the elderly women of Galisteo had died and bathing at dawn was abandoned. Originally, the men of the town had bathed after the women.

26. Espinosa, "New Mexican Spanish Folklore," 416.

27. Frances Toor, *A Treasury of Mexican Folkways* (New York: Crown Publishers, 1957), 233.

28. Personal communication, Nasario García to Marc Simmons, Las Vegas, New Mexico, 10 September 1999.

29. Personal communication, Orlando Romero to Marc Simmons, Nambé, New Mexico, 11 November 1999. On the antiquity of re-baptism as a renewal rite in the Christian tradition, see, William Wroth, "La Sangre de Cristo: History and Symbolism," in Marta Weigle, ed., *Hispanic Arts and Ethnohistory in the Southwest* (Santa Fe: Ancient City Press, 1983), 290.

30. For a discussion of gift and water throwing, see, Lange, "San Juan's Day at Cochiti Pueblo," 180–81.

31. Toor, *A Treasury of Mexican Folkways,* 233.

32. WPA typescript, "Native Customs and Celebrations," #36.

33. WPA typescript, "St. John's Day," #36; and, Jaramillo, *Shadows of the Past,* 85–86.

34. Abe Peña, "San Juan Bautista," undated typescript in possession of the author.

35. Josephine Barela, *Ojo de Gallo, A Nostalgic Narrative of Historic San Rafael* (Santa Fe: Sleeping Fox, 1975), 17.

36. Brenan, *South From Granada,* 127; and, Ortiz y Pino de Kleven interview. The chorus at Galisteo, after singing in the street, was invited into the houses of the Juanes for hot chocolate.

37. Elsie Clews Parsons, *The Pueblo of Isleta* (reprint ed., Albuquerque: Calvin Horn Publisher, 1974), 289. Placing the first rooster on the altar may be a holdover from New Mexico's colonial days when citizens made an annual voluntary offering to the Church of their first fruits (*primicias*), that is, the initial increase in livestock or products yielded by the fields. That the Isletans gave gifts of bread and goat cheese is probably a coincidence and unrelated to the custom of young people in Spain going into the fields to feast on ring bread (*roscas*) and white cheese.

38. McDermott, *Travels in Search of the Elephant,* 125.

39. WPA typescript, "El Gallo," #389; and, Rubén Cobos, *A Dictionary of New Mexico and Southern Colorado Spanish* (Santa Fe: Museum of New Mexico Press, 1983), 75. Compare the definition here of *gallo* as meaning "invitation" with that of the word *convite*. See also, Jaramillo, *Shadows of the Past,* 87, on the *convite*.

40. Peña, "San Juan Bautista," typescript; and, Olibama López Tushar, *The People of El Valle,* 115.

41. For Lt. William H. Emory's comment on this matter, see Ross Calvin, ed., *Lt. Emory Reports* (Albuquerque: University of New Mexico Press, 1968), 59.

42. McDermott, *Travels in Search of the Elephant,* 126.

43. Archivo General de la Nación, Mexico, Provincias Internas, vol. 35, exp. 6, as cited in Vina Walz, "History of the El Paso Area, 1680–1692" (unpublished Ph.D. diss., University of New Mexico, 1951), 242n.

44. Gregg, *Commerce of the Prairies,* 169; and, Adams and Chávez, *The Missions of New Mexico, 1776,* 241.

45. Charles F. Lummis, *A New Mexico David* (New York: Charles Scribners' Sons, 1891), 148.

46. Elsie Clews Parsons, *Pueblo Indian Religion,* 2 vols. (Chicago: University of Chicago Press, 1939), 2: 1108.

47. WPA typescript, "Life in the Old Houses: Fiesta Days," #21; and, Ruth Laughlin Barker, *Caballeros* (New York: D. Appleton-Century Co., 1936), 198.

48. Gregg, *Commerce of the Prairies,* 169.

49. Jaramillo, *Shadows of the Past,* 86.

50. Abe Peña, *Memories of Cíbola* (Albuquerque: University of New Mexico Press, 1997), 191. Lt. John G. Bourke mentioned seeing Navajos joining in the corrida at Santo Domingo on the Rio Grande in 1881. *Snake Dance of the Moquis* (reprint ed., Tucson: University of Arizona Press, 1984), 51.

51. Peña, *Memories of Cíbola,* 191; and, WPA typescript, "A Corrida de Gallo at San José," # 51.

52. Marta Weigle and Peter White, *The Lore of New Mexico* (Albuquerque: University of New Mexico Press, 1988), 399.

53. Gregg, 170.

54. Arthur L. Campa, *Hispanic Culture in the Southwest* (Norman: University of Oklahoma Press, 1979), 193; and WPA typescript, "Life in the Old Houses," #21.

55. Bourke, *Snake Dance of the Moquis,* 52.

56. The phenomenon of the *galleras* (female rooster pullers) is scarcely mentioned in the literature. No eyewitness account of their participation has thus far come to light.

57. Tushar, *The People of El Valle,* 116.

58. Barela, *Ojo de Gallo,* 18; and, Weigle and White, *The Lore of New Mexico,* 494, n. 63.

59. WPA typescript, "Life in the Old Houses," #21; and, John G. Bourke, "Notes on the Language and Folk-Usage of the Rio Grande Valley," *Journal of American Folklore* 9 (April 1896): 102; and, Lummis, *A New Mexico David,* 155.

60. Parsons, *Pueblo Indian Religion,* 2: 1108. On blood as an ingredient in rain-making ceremonies, see Frazer, *The Golden Bough,* 74–75.

61. Leslie A. White, *The Pueblo of Santo Domingo, New Mexico* (Millwood, N.Y.: Kraus Reprint Co., 1974), 157–58.

62. Lummis, *Mesa, Cañon and Pueblo,* 209.

63. Frazer, *The Golden Bough,* 73.

64. Ortiz y Pino de Kleven interview, 1 September 1999.

CHAPTER 11

1. For an overview of the Spanish expulsion from Mexico, see, Harold D. Sims, *La expulsión de los españoles de México, 1821–1828* (Mexico: Fondo de Cultura Económica, 1974); and, Sims, "Los exiliados españoles de México in 1829," *Historia Mexicana* 30 (January–March 1981): 391–416. Also, Romeo Flores Caballero, *La contrarevolución en la independencia* (Mexico: El Colegio de México, 1969).

2. Luis Miguel Díaz and Jaime G. Martini, comps., *Relaciones diplomáticas: México-España (1821–1977)* (Mexico: Editorial Porrúa, 1977), 59.

3. Díaz and Martini, *Relaciones diplomáticas,* 60.

4. Carlos Alvear Acevedo, *Historia de México* (1964: 2nd revised ed., Mexico: Editorial Jus, 1965), 216, 227; and, José C. Valadés, *Orígenes de la república mexicana* (Mexico: Impresiones Rodas, 1972), 102.

5. Díaz and Martini, *Relaciones diplomáticas,* 61–63.

6. Report on the Missions of New Mexico, unsigned, n.p., 19 March 1789, Biblioteca Nacional, México, leg. 10, no. 85.

7. David J. Weber reports twenty-five Spanish-born friars serving in California in the same period. *The Mexican Frontier, 1821–1846* (Albuquerque: University of New Mexico Press, 1982), 45. He also notes (p. 74) that New Mexico had eight secular priests in 1829.

8. Daniel Tyler, "New Mexico in the 1820s: The First Administration of Manuel Armijo" (Ph.D. diss., University of New Mexico, 1971), 250.

9. Proceedings Against Spanish Priests, Santa Fe, 5–13 February 1828, Mexican Archives of New Mexico (MANM), SRCA, Santa Fe; and, Kessell, *Kiva, Cross and Crown,* 454.

10. Proceedings Against Spanish Priests, Santa Fe, 5–13 February 1828, MANM.

11. Ibid., Santa Fe, 5–13 February 1828, MANM.

12. Ibid., Santa Fe, 7–9 February 1828, MANM.

13. José Antonio Arce to Supremo Gobierno, Chihuahua, 1828, Ramo Expulsión de los Españoles, vol. 24, exp. 1, f. 1–35, Archivo General de la Nación (AGN), Mexico, cited in, Rogelio López Espinoza, comp., *Catálogo del ramo expulsión de españoles,* 2 vols. (Guide no. 26, Mexico: AGN, n.d.), 1: 75. Reference courtesy of Daniel Tyler. This *ramo* contains a total of seventy-two volumes of documents and includes proceedings, appeals, and judgments relating to the status of Spaniards throughout Mexico.

14. Notices to Governors, in, Proceedings Against Spanish Citizens, Santa Fe, 11–13 February 1828, MANM.

15. Tyler, "New Mexico in the 1820s," 261. The notice of Bengochea's seditious activities may, in fact, have been untrue. At least, later in 1828, he protested his expulsion in a case entitled, "D. Benito Samada de Bengochea sobre haber sido expulsado de Nuevo México como español, siendo mexicano," Espinoza, *Catálogo del ramo expulsión de españoles,* 1: 20.

16. Proceedings Against Spanish Citizens, Santa Fe, 7–9 February 1828, MANM.

17. Tyler, "New Mexico in the 1820s," 253–54; and, Proceedings Against the Spaniard Atanacio Bolíbar, Santa Fe, 23–27 September 1827, MANM.

18. Espinoza, *Catálogo del ramo expulsión de españoles,* 1: 14.

19. Chávez, *Archives, 1678–1900,* 243; and, Espinoza, *Catálogo del ramo expulsión de españoles,* 1: 57.

20. Espinoza, 1: 60.

21. L. Bradford Prince, *Historical Sketches of New Mexico* (Kansas City: Ramsey, Millet, & Hudson, 1883), 233.

22. Ralph Emerson Twitchell, *The Leading Facts of New Mexican History,* 5 vols. (Cedar Rapids, Iowa: Torch Press, 1911), 2: 55.

23. Díaz and Martini, *Relaciones diplomáticas,* 64–65.

24. Sims, "Los exiliados españoles," 392–97.

25. Notice of the Number of Spaniards Expelled from New Mexico, Santa Fe, 20 November 1829, Misc. Documents, MANM. Alvarez served as consul from 1839 to 1846. On his life, see Harold H. Dunham, "Manuel Alvarez," in LeRoy R. Hafen, ed., *The Mountain Men and the Fur Trade of the Far West*, 10 vols. (Glendale, Calif.: Arthur H. Clark Co., 1965–1972), 1: 180–97. Therein, Dunham notes (p. 184), "Sometime during the later 1820s, Alvarez decided to enter the Rocky Mountain fur trade; just when or how is not clear." It now appears that Alvarez's expulsion from New Mexico in 1829 led him to join the fur traders. He was probably the same "*ibérico* Manuel Alvarez" who submitted documents that same year to the central government in Mexico City asking that he not be expelled for health reasons (Espinoza, *Catálogo del ramo expulsión de españoles*, 1: 94). Claims of poor health, many of them obviously contrived, was the principal excuse advanced by the many Spaniards who asked that their sentences of expulsion be set aside. See also Thomas E. Chávez, "The Life and Times of Manuel Alvarez, 1794–1856" (Ph.D. diss., University of New Mexico, 1980), 13–14.

26. Notice of the Number of Spaniards Expelled from New Mexico, Santa Fe, 20 November 1829, Misc. Documents, MANM.

27. Tyler, "New Mexico in the 1820s," 258; and, José M. Ponce de León, *Reseñas históricas del estado de Chihuahua* (2nd edition, Chihuahua: Imprenta del Gobierno, 1913), 206–12.

28. *Niles' Register*, 21 March 1829.

29. *Niles' Register*, 23 May 1829.

30. Milton Bryan, "The Flight of Time: Adventures on the Plains Sixty Years Ago" (typescript, Topeka: Kansas State Historical Society Collections, 1887), 9.

31. A list of the members of the caravan as it left Santa Fe, translated from the Spanish, is provided by Otis E. Young, *The First Military Escort on The Santa Fe trail* (Glendale, Calif.: Arthur H. Clark Co., 1952), 142, 194.

32. Fred S. Perrine, "Military Escorts on the Santa Fe Trail," *NMHR* 2 (April 1927): 191.

33. Philip St. George Cooke, *Scenes and Adventures in the Army: or, Romance of Military Life* (Philadelphia: Lindsay & Blakiston, 1857), 86.

34. *Missouri Intelligencer*, 1 November 1829.

35. Gregg, *Commerce of the Prairies*, 33.

36. Rafael Chacón, "Memoirs, 1833–1846" (typescript, Boulder: University of Colorado Historical Collections, 1912), 14. Reference courtesy of Janet Lecompte.

37. John Francis McDermott, ed., "Alfred S. Waugh's 'Desultory Wanderings in the Years 1845–46,'" *Bulletin of the Missouri Historical Society* 7 (April 1951): 363. For another case of a Spaniard mistreated by New Mexicans, see Gregg, 121.

38. Quoted in Alvear Acevedo, *Historia de México*, 227. Normal diplomatic relations were not restored between Mexico and Spain until 18 December 1836 (Flores Caballero, *La contrarevolución*, 149).

SELECTED REFERENCES

Baxter, John O. *Las Carneradas, Sheep Trade in New Mexico, 1700–1860.* Albuquerque: University of New Mexico Press, 1987. One of the few specialized studies on New Mexico's pastoral economy.

Brown, Lorin W. *Hispano Folklife of New Mexico.* Albuquerque: University of New Mexico Press, 1978. Traditional Hispanic ways of living that survived into the 1930s, as recorded in the Federal Writers' Project Manuscripts.

Carlson, Alvar W. *The Spanish-American Homeland, Four Centuries in New Mexico's Río Arriba Country.* Baltimore: Johns Hopkins University Press, 1990. The author attempts to show how cultural and social factors entrapped New Mexicans in a subsistence economy.

Colligan, John B. *The Juan Páez Hurtado Expedition of 1695.* Albuquerque: University of New Mexico Press, 1995. This close examination of a colonizing expedition reveals much about society at the end of the seventeenth century, and about material culture.

Cutter, Charles R. *The Protector de Indios in Colonial New Mexico, 1659–1821.* Albuquerque: University of New Mexico Press, 1986. Describes in insightful detail Indian interactions with the Spanish legal system.

Espinosa, Aurelio M. *The Folklore of Spain in the American Southwest.* Norman: University of Oklahoma Press, 1985. A comprehensive treatment of New Mexico's folk literature by a native scholar.

Hall, Thomas D. *Social Change in the Southwest, 1350–1880.* Lawrence: University Press of Kansas, 1989. The evolution of colonial New Mexico from the perspective of a sociologist.

Kessell, John L. *Kiva, Cross, and Crown*. Washington, D.C.: National Park Service, 1979. This history of Pecos Pueblo discloses the cross-fertilization that occurred between the societies of Indian and Spaniard.

————. *Remote Beyond Compare, Letters of don Diego de Vargas to his Family from New Spain and New Mexico, 1675–1706*. Albuquerque: University of New Mexico Press, 1989. These rare personal letters give clues to the interior world of a major colonial figure.

Nostrand, Richard L. *The Hispano Homeland*. Norman: University of Oklahoma Press, 1992. A geographer's view, giving special attention to Hispano migration patterns and their impact on social and economic conditions.

Palmer, Gabrielle G., comp. *El Camino Real de Tierra Adentro*. 2 vols. Santa Fe: Bureau of Land Management, 1989, 1999. The Camino Real was New Mexico's artery of communication with the outside world, its traffic and goods shaping the character of colonial life.

Steele, Thomas J., et al., eds. *Seeds of Struggle, Harvest of Faith*. Albuquerque: LPD Press, 1998. Colonial New Mexicans cannot be understood without reference to their Catholic faith, here illuminated in a series of essays published on the 400th anniversary of the Church's establishment on the upper Rio Grande.

Van Ness, John R. *Hispanos in Northern New Mexico*. New York: AMS Press, 1991. Analytical study of traditional village life.

Weckmann, Luís. *The Medieval Heritage of Mexico*. New York: Fordham University Press, 1992. In the medieval legacy, one can find numerous influences shaping the society of New Mexico's Hispanic colonists.

Westphall, Victor. *Mercedes Reales, Hispanic Land Grants of the Upper Rio Grande Region*. Albuquerque: University of New Mexico Press, 1983. Spanish land grants affected colonial society and economic issues at every turn, as this overview clearly shows.

ACKNOWLEDGMENTS

I am grateful to publishers and journals credited here for permission to include in this book pieces I've written over the years.

"Introduction," *Colonial Frontiers* (Santa Fe: Ancient City Press, 1983).

"The Pueblo Revolt: Why Did It Happen?" *El Palacio*, 86 (winter 1980–1981).

"Misery as a Factor in Colonial Life," Anne V. Poore, ed., *Reflections: Papers on Southwestern Culture History in Honor of Charles H. Lange*, Archeological Society of New Mexico, 14 (Santa Fe: Ancient City Press, 1988).

"The Founding of Albuquerque: Another Look," *New Mexico Historical Review*, 55 (July 1980).

"Colonial Physicians," Previously unpublished.

"The Great Smallpox Epidemic, 1780–1781," *New Mexico Historical Review*, 41 (October 1966).

"Origins of Public Health," *New Mexico Historical Review*, 67 (July 1992).

"Attempts to Open a New Mexico-Sonora Road," *Arizona and the West*, 17 (spring 1975).

"The Rise of Cattle Ranching," *El Palacio*, 93 (spring 1988).

"Water That Runs in Ditches," *New Mexico Historical Review*, 47 (April 1972).

"St. John's Day: Remnant of an Ancient Festival," Previously unpublished.

"The Spanish Exiles," *New Mexico Historical Review*, 59 (January 1984).

INDEX

Page numbers in *italics* refer to illustrations.